DATE DUE

JAN 03 2004		
FEB 2 0 2014		

DEMCO 38-296

CULTURES OF THE WORLD®

NEPAL

Jon Burbank

BENCHMARK BOOKS

MARSHALL CAVENDISH
NEW YORK

PICTURE CREDITS

Cover photo: © Trip/W. Jacobs

Noazesh Ahmed: 13, 124 • APA: 5 • Liz Berryman: 79, 80, 88, 110 • Jon Burbank: 3, 4, 8, 9, 10, 11, 12, 15, 20, 21, 23, 24, 25, 26, 28, 29, 33, 34, 35, 38, 39, 41, 42, 43, 45 46, 47, 48, 49, 50, 51, 52, 53, 54, 55, 57, 58, 59, 60, 61, 62, 63, 64, 65, 67, 68, 69, 72, 73, 75, 77, 81, 82, 84, 89, 92, 93, 94, 95, 96, 97, 98, 99, 100, 103, 104, 106, 107, 109, 111, 112, 113, 114, 115, 116, 117, 118, 119, 120, 121, 123, 125, 127, 128, 130, 131 • Joginder Chawla: 19, 86, 122 • Haga Library, Japan: 18 • Earl Kowall: 6, 31, 36, 37, 108 • Earl & Nazima Kowall: 40 • Life File Photo Library: 14, 16, 70 • Christine Osborne: 30 • Dominic Sansoni: 32, 90 • Bernard Sonneville: 66 • Travel Ink: 56, 102 • Alison Wright: title, 44

ACKNOWLEDGMENTS

With thanks to the Consulate-General of the Kingdom of Nepal in Singapore for their expert reading of this manuscript.

PRECEDING PAGE

The Kumari, accompanied by a few children, takes a peek at the outside world from her palace window.

Marshall Cavendish Corporation
99 White Plains Road
Tarrytown, NY 10591
Website: www.marshallcavendish.com

© 1990, 2002 by Times Media Private Limited
All rights reserved. First edition 1990. Second edition 2002.

Originated and designed by
Times Books International, an imprint of
Times Media Private Limited, a member of the
Times Publishing Group

Printed in Malaysia

Library of Congress Cataloging-in-Publication Data
Burbank, Jon, 1951–
    Nepal / Jon Burbank.—2nd ed.
        p. cm.—(Cultures of the world)
    Summary: Describes the geography, history, government, economy, people, religion, language, and culture of Nepal, a predominantly Hindu country located north of India. Includes several recipes.
    Includes bibliographical references and index.
    ISBN 0-7614-1476-2
    1. Nepal—Juvenile literature. [1. Nepal.] I. Title. II. Series.
DS 493.4 .B87 2002
954.96—dc21   2002025994

7 6 5 4 3

CONTENTS

This Tamang man comes from one of the many hill tribes in Nepal. The Tamang often come down from their homes to the Kathmandu Valley in search of work.

In the higher areas, a great deal of domestic life takes place on the rooftops of houses. It's the best place to dry crops and to bask in the warm sunshine.

INTRODUCTION

MOST PEOPLE KNOW NEPAL as the home of Mount Everest, the world's tallest mountain. The Himalayan mountain range that stretches across Nepal's northern border includes eight of the 10 tallest mountains in the world. Nepal houses many important pilgrimage sites for Hindus, including Janakpur, the site where the great hero Ram won the hand of his wife Sita. Nepal's official religion is Hinduism, but there is also a strong Buddhist element. The historical Buddha, Siddhartha Gautama, was born in the Nepalese town of Lumbini, near the border with India.

Living on mountain sides and in narrow valleys are dozens of ethnic groups, speaking different languages and worshiping different gods. Somehow, all these groups have lived together for years in peace. Although Nepal is ranked as one of the poorest and least developed countries in the world, its mix of ancient cultures and awe-inspiring physical beauty makes it one of the world's richest and most fascinating places on earth.

GEOGRAPHY

MILLIONS OF YEARS AGO, the earth had only one immense land mass, which scientists have called Pangaea. Eventually this supercontinent broke up, and over time, the pieces moved apart and then recombined in different ways until they began to resemble the continents we recognize today. This movement of tectonic plates is ongoing and continues to cause geographic changes.

Nepal's story began about 10–15 million years ago when present-day India was a separate continent, not attached to Asia but slowly moving toward it. When the two land masses finally collided, the pressure that resulted pushed the edges of the two continents up, forming majestic mountains and a series of hills below the mountains. Thus Nepal was born.

Nepal is a landlocked country, surrounded by Tibet and China in the north and India in the south. It has an area of 56,139 square miles (147,180 square km) with a population of 25.3 million people.

Although 85 percent of Nepal is mountainous, the country can be divided into three geographic regions: the towering Himalayan mountain range, the cool terraces and valleys that form the Middle Hills, and the warm, humid lowlands of the *terai* ("teh-RYE").

Opposite: **Nepal is home to the Himalayas, the tallest and youngest mountain range in the world.**

Below: **The subcontinent of India used to be part of southern Africa, Australia, and Antarctica. The movement of the earth's crust over millions of years pushed these lands apart, and India fused with the Asian continent.**

THE HIMALAYAS

Along trade routes in the mountains, caravans of horses are used to transport goods from one town to another. The steep and rugged geography of Nepal makes it difficult and impractical to build roads.

Himalaya comes from two words in Sanskrit, one of the oldest languages in the world. *Hima* means "snow" and *alaya* means "abode." This is not surprising as the Himalayan mountains are covered with snow throughout the year. The range stretches across the whole northern part of Nepal.

About 33 percent of Nepal's land is at altitudes over 10,000 feet (3,048 m). Almost 10 percent of the population lives at these elevations, working as traders, herders, and farmers. Barley, millet, and potatoes are among the few crops that can grow at altitudes of up to 14,000 feet (4,267 m).

The climate in the Himalayan region is cold, with snowfalls in winter. Because of the high altitude, there is less oxygen in the air than at lower altitudes. Visitors who are not used to living in high places may develop altitude sickness, which can be fatal unless they return to lower altitudes.

MOUNT EVEREST

Worldwide there are only 14 mountain peaks over 26,247 feet (8,000 m). Eight of the 10 tallest mountains are in Nepal, including Mount Everest, the tallest at 29,022 feet (8,850 m).

Despite numerous attempts, no climbers scaled Mount Everest until Sir Edmund Hillary and Tenzing Norgay, a Sherpa guide, finally reached the top in 1953. In 1978 Rheinold Messner and his partner Peter Habler were the first to climb it without using bottled oxygen.

At different times, other mountain peaks were thought to hold the title of highest in the world. Dhaulagiri, Kanchenjunga, and Gauri Shankar (visible from the Kathmandu Valley) were all once thought to hold the crown.

In 1863, when India was ruled by Britain, a survey done by the Indian Survey Office confirmed Everest as the tallest mountain in the world. On the Tibetan side, Everest is called Chomolungma and on the Nepali side, Sagarmatha. Both names mean "mother of the world." The surveyors, unaware of these names, first called it Peak 15, and then Everest, after a former head of the survey office.

In the mid-1980s Everest's position as the tallest mountain in the world was challenged when a geographer claimed that Mount K2 in Pakistan was taller, but measurements using laser and satellite technology confirmed Everest as the tallest. This was confirmed in 1999 by two American climbers supported by five Sherpa guides.

A typical village in the Middle Hills. Terraced fields have been carved out of the hillsides for growing rice, barley, beans, and millet.

THE MIDDLE HILLS

Half of Nepal lies in an area called the Mahabharat Range, or the Middle Hills, and just under 50 percent of the population lives here. The height of these hills varies from 5,000 to 12,000 feet (1,524 to 3,658 m), so calling them "hills" is a little misleading, because almost anywhere else in the world they would be called mountains. Mount Kosciusko, the highest mountain in Australia, is 7,310 feet (2,228 m) tall.

Seen from the air, the Middle Hills resemble a series of endless steep ridges. Over the centuries, the Nepalese have built steep terraces on these hills in order to grow food.

The rugged landscape makes it almost impossible to build roads, so Nepalese almost always travel by foot. Distances are not measured by miles, but by the hours or days it takes to walk to a destination. Men, women, and children all carry food, school books, and medical supplies on their backs to their destinations.

The Middle Hills

The Middle Hills, once crowned with thick, luxuriant forests, are becoming more and more barren. Villagers depend on the forests for fodder, firewood, and building materials. As the population increases, trees are being cut faster than they can be replaced. Unfortunately, the loss of foliage causes village water supplies to dry up, and soil erosion eats away at the hillsides.

There are several large valleys scattered among the hills. The largest one is the Pokhara Valley in central Nepal. The most famous valley, however, is Kathmandu Valley, 124 miles (200 km) east of Pokhara.

Ask people in the Middle Hills traveling to Kathmandu where they are going, and chances are the answer will be "Nepal." For many, Kathmandu is Nepal.

A picturesque Nepalese village. Life in a village is difficult, without health clinics, running water, telephones, electricity, or other modern facilities.

THE KATHMANDU VALLEY

The Kathmandu Valley has always been the heart of Nepal. Although only about 450 square miles (1,166 square km) in land area, it is home to over one million people. The valley lies at an elevation of 4,383 feet (1,336 m), which gives it a mild climate. Temperatures rarely go above 86°F (30°C) in the hot season, and in winter the temperature rarely falls below 32°F (0°C).

The capital city of Kathmandu has a population of over 500,000 people. It was founded by King Gunakamadeva in the eighth century. The name Kathmandu was derived from a temple built in the 10th century in the city called Kasthamandap.

Kathmandu's rapid growth has caused serious environmental problems. The air quality in the city is considered among the worst in the world, and there is a severe shortage of water. Garbage and industrial waste also threaten the environment.

THE TERAI

Nepal's only flat area is a narrow strip along the southern border with India. This strip is called the *terai*. Because it forms part of the flood plain of the Ganges River in northern India, the *terai* is very fertile.

The *terai* used to be covered with thick jungle and was uninhabitable because of malaria, a disease spread by mosquitoes. In the 1950s the World Health Organization (WHO) sponsored a program to spray large tracts of the *terai* with the pesticide DDT. The malaria was brought under control, and hill people began to settle the area.

The *terai* quickly changed into Nepal's bread basket and rice bowl. It is also the center for what little industry Nepal has.

Today, the *terai is* home to over 50 percent of the population, although it forms only 15 percent of Nepal's land area. Every year, people from the Middle Hills migrate here at an increasing rate.

The climate in the *terai* is extremely hot, with temperatures in the summer (April to June) reaching 100°F (38°C). A deadly wind called the *loo* ("loo"), with temperatures of over 112°F (44°C), sometimes kills people in the fields. The heavy monsoon rains from June to September bring cooler temperatures and rain to the rice fields.

Most of Nepal's rice is grown in the *terai*. Few machines are used for farming. Instead, animals are often used to plow the land.

Ice and snow from the mountains feed Nepal's rivers and streams.

RIVERS

Nepal has thousands of streams, which flow down mountains and hillsides into hundreds of rivers. Yet out of those hundreds of rivers, only three are strong enough to cut through the Middle Hills down to the *terai* and on to the dusty plains of India. These three rivers are the Kosi in the east, the Kali in the center, and the Karnali in the west.

During the monsoon, the heavy rains cause the rivers to overflow. There are few bridges in Nepal, and most are washed away yearly by flood waters. Flooding rivers can sweep away houses, even whole villages.

Still, the rivers are Nepal's only natural resource. They have tremendous hydroelectric potential, but building and maintaining hydroelectric plants in Nepal's rugged landscape would be difficult and expensive. The cost of the electricity produced would be so high that most Nepalese would not be able to afford electricity. Projects where a small hydroelectric plant provides electricity for a small village have proven more effective.

FLORA

The extremes of altitude in Nepal create a variety of climates and environments that support a fascinating variety of plants.

The rhododendron is the national flower of Nepal. The rhododendron tree can be found at altitudes up to 9,000 feet (2,743 m).

In the *terai,* sal, a hardwood, is the dominant tree. Sal provides excellent timber for building homes and furniture.

In the Middle Hills, there are pines, alders, oaks, hemlock, birches, and forests of evergreens such as juniper. There are also many forests of large rhododendron trees in the east and center of the country.

The bright red rhododendron blossom is Nepal's national flower. Entire hillsides turn red in the spring when the rhododendron forests bloom; this is one of Nepal's most beautiful sights.

Nepal's forests provide over 35 percent of all the energy used in the country. The use of the trees for energy needs is a major cause of deforestation in Nepal. One report says 3 percent of Nepal's forests are disappearing every year. Once a section of hillside is logged, the monsoon rains wash away the topsoil into the rivers, which eventually carry it as far as the Bay of Bengal. Without this fertile soil, nothing can grow on the hills.

The Nepalese government is working with foreign aid agencies to foster community forestry projects. Each village is responsible for replenishing its own forest by growing tree nurseries. Still, it takes a generation to replace what is cut down in a few minutes.

Yaks are the beasts of burden in the Himalayas for the simple reason that they can live at high altitudes. If yaks travel below 7,000 feet (2,133 m), they get reverse altitude sickness, which can be fatal to them.

ANIMAL LIFE

Bengal tigers, rhinoceros, leopards, buffalo, bears, monkeys, and all kinds of smaller mammals dwell in the jungles of the lowlands, especially in the national parks. Nepal also has two species of crocodile: gharial have a needle-shaped snout and eat mostly fish; muggers have big snouts, and can grow 10 feet (3.5 m) long.

Nepal's most reclusive resident is the rare snow leopard. Little was known about this beautiful silver and black cat until recently. They are solitary and elusive and live in the high Himalayan region.

There are ongoing conservation programs to rebuild the populations of tigers, rhinoceros, and gharials, which are all threatened with extinction. Not everyone, however, is in favor of the conservation programs. Farmers suffer terrible damage from these animals. Tigers and leopards eat livestock and, occasionally, humans. Rhinoceros can ruin a farmer's entire crop in one night. A troop of monkeys will eat through a field in an hour. It comes as no surprise then that most Nepalese feel they are competing with the same animals others are trying to save.

THE YETI

Nepal's most famous resident, the yeti (also called the Abominable Snowman) may not exist at all. The Sherpas, who share its habitat, call it the "yet-tch" and have even distinguished two different types: one that eats cattle and another that eats people.

The yeti was dismissed as a legend until a British army major, L.A. Waddell, found huge footprints in the snow in 1889. In 1921 the leader of an Everest expedition reported seeing a dark creature walking in the snow and found some strange footprints.

The yeti has managed to elude discovery despite numerous expeditions sent to capture it. The famous mountain climber Eric Shipton found a set of footprints in 1951 that prompted several expeditions, including one led by Sir Edmund Hillary, the first conqueror of Everest.

Interest in the yeti died down after a series of disappointments. A supposed yeti scalp was taken from the Pangboche Monastery for tests and identified as belonging to a mountain goat. Most of the pictures of yeti footprints were found to be small bird and rodent tracks that had melted in the sun.

Interest rose again in 1974 when a Sherpa woman was allegedly attacked by a yeti, who also killed several of her yaks.

What does a yeti look like? Tall, perhaps taller than a person, with orange fur, and a pointed head. Some reports say its feet point backwards. One theory claims that it belongs to a species of giant orangutans that was thought extinct. Until one is actually found, however, the identity of the yeti will remain a mystery.

HISTORY

NEPAL'S EARLY HISTORY began in the Kathmandu Valley, which was once a lake. Geologists believe that the lake drained about 200,000 years ago, but the cause is unclear. Legend says that the god Manjushri sliced the valley wall at Chohar, where there is a narrow gorge, and drained the water.

The Hindu god Indra is said to have visited the valley of Kathmandu in the seventh or eighth century B.C. disguised as a human. There, Indra met with the king. Siddharta Gautama, the founder of Buddhism, was born about 563 B.C. in Lumbini, a town located on the plains of Nepal's *terai*. He is also believed to have visited Kathmandu during his travels.

Although much of the country's history is shrouded in myth, it is certain that by the time of the Licchavi Dynasty, Nepal's first golden age around A.D. 300, the religions of Hinduism and Buddhism had been firmly established. During those years, visitors from Chinese kingdoms marveled at the richness of the king's palace and courtyards. When the last Licchavi king died in A.D. 733, Nepal plunged into its dark age.

Above: **A portrait of King Prithvi Narayan Shah, known as the "Father of the Nation." His military conquests united the warring states of Nepal.**

Opposite: **The splendor of Nepal's architecture reflects a history of rich and advanced cultural traditions.**

THE GREEN TARA

One of the most significant legacies of Nepal was its introduction of Buddhism to Tibet.

A Nepalese princess, Bhirkhuti, was given in marriage to the powerful Tibetan king Tsrong Gompo. The king was the strongest, fiercest warrior of his day. He and his army were so feared that even the powerful Chinese sent a princess in marriage as a sign of respect. Bhirkuti's faith, however, was strong enough to convert the king and Tibet to Buddhism.

Bhirkuti is still loved in Tibet and worshiped as the Green Tara, a symbol of mercy and compassion. She is also worshiped by Buddhists in Nepal.

The pagodas of Patan. In the 16th century, Patan was one of three rich kingdoms occupying the Kathmandu Valley.

THE MALLAS

In 1200, the Malla Dynasty was established. Although the early Malla kings were strict Hindus, they established a tradition of peaceful coexistence with the Buddhists; this tradition is still strong today. The Malla kings were also able administrators who codified the Hindu caste system.

During the first three centuries of Malla rule, the valley endured many invasions from western Nepalese and Muslims from northern India. As many as 80 small kingdoms in what is now Nepal fought each other to increase the size of their kingdoms. Muslims from Bengal did actually take over the valley in 1364. The Mallas regained control within a week, however, and the short Muslim occupation of the kingdom had no lasting influence.

The Mallas in the Kathmandu Valley prospered, and Nepal's second golden age began in the 15th century. The valley's three main cities, Kathmandu, Bhaktapur, and Patan, grew wealthy on the trade between India and Tibet. Most of the sculptures, woodcarvings, and buildings the valley is famous for today were built during this time.

Yaksha Malla was the greatest of the Malla kings. He ruled a kingdom far bigger than present-day Nepal. His kingdom was divided among his

three sons. Their quarrels split the small Kathmandu Valley into three kingdoms—Kathmandu, Patan, and Bhaktapur. For the next 200 years, each kingdom built fine palaces, but their rulers—all cousins— schemed against one another, eventually causing their own downfall.

Prithvi Narayan Shah's castle in Gorkha. It was from this hilltop fortress that he began the conquest of the Kathmandu Valley.

THE HOUSE OF SHAH

Sixty miles (96.5 km) west of Kathmandu, Prithvi Narayan Shah, king of the small Rajput kingdom of Gorkha, watched the bickering of Kathmandu's four kings and decided to strike. He was a brave man, a good leader and strategist, and a good politician. He was also persistent: it took him more than 20 years to take Kathmandu. To his good fortune, even after he attacked the valley, the Malla kings refused to join as one army and fight back. Through battles and political intrigue, Prithvi Narayan Shah conquered the kingdoms one by one. In 1768 he became sole king of Kathmandu.

Prithvi Narayan Shah and his successors expanded the kingdom until it included Sikkim in the east and a small area of Kashmir in the west. By the early 1800s, Nepal was one of the greatest powers in South Asia.

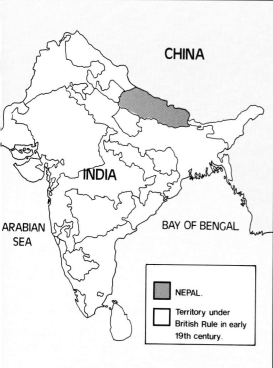

The British occupation of India in the early part of the 19th century.

CHINA

INDIA

ARABIAN SEA

BAY OF BENGAL

NEPAL.

Territory under British Rule in early 19th century.

THE BRITISH

Nepal's expansion brought it into contact with the other expanding power of the time—Britain. In 1814 Nepal and Britain went to war over a territorial dispute. After some initial success on the Nepalese side, the British triumphed. The British forced Nepal to sign a treaty in 1816. This treaty reduced the country almost to its present size and gave Britain the right to station a representative in Kathmandu.

Irritated by the treaty they were forced to sign, the Nepalese gave the British representative the worst land in the valley, which was infested with malaria and "evil spirits." They also denied him the right to leave the valley except to go to and from India by a single route.

The experience left Nepal so resentful of foreigners that it closed its borders until 1951.

THE KOT MASSACRE

Nepal's defeat by the British threw the government into turmoil. Because of the treaty, ambitious members of the aristocracy had no opportunity to expand Nepal further. So they turned against each other instead and formed factions in a political war for control of Nepal.

In 1846 the queen's lover was murdered during a palace intrigue. The furious queen gathered the various squabbling factions together in her *kot* ("koht"), meaning "fort," and accusations and insults flew. Hands reached for swords, and by the next morning, several dominant families had been wiped out. Jang Bahadur Rana, one of the faction leaders, survived.

Rana appointed himself prime minister, and he and his family ruled

In 1850, Jang Bahadur Rana became the first Nepalese leader to travel to Britain and France. His family ruled Nepal for over 100 years.

Nepal for the next 115 years. The king was reduced to a mere puppet on the throne. The Ranas did nothing to improve the country and the lives of the people. When the Ranas were overthrown in 1951, only 5 percent of Nepal's population knew how to read and write.

THE RESTORATION OF MONARCHY

After India gained independence in 1947, pressure grew in Nepal for the Ranas to reform the government. There were even protests and strikes at factories in the *terai*. The opposition was led by the able and charismatic B.P. Koirala, who operated from a base in India. In 1950, the king seized the initiative to depose the Ranas and restore the authority of the royal family. He first requested asylum in the Indian Embassy in Kathmandu.

King Tribhuvan was flown to India, where he demanded that the Ranas return power to him and the people of Nepal. The Ranas responded by declaring his crown null and void and appointing Tribhuvan's infant grandson king. All international governments refused to recognize the new infant king and expressed their support for King Tribhuvan.

Above: **The late King Birendra and Queen Aishwarya toss coins to dancers at a festival. The king and queen, along with most members of the royal family, were allegedly murdered by their son, the late Crown Prince Dipendra.**

Opposite: **The Ranas used the wealth of Nepal to benefit themselves by building palaces and living a life of luxury. This Rana palace has since been converted to a college dormitory.**

DEMOCRACY IN NEPAL

Tribhuvan declared his support for a democratic government. With popular support, the king took control of Nepal within a year. King Tribhuvan laid the foundation for parliamentary democracy before his death in 1955. In 1959 a constitution was adopted, and the first democratic election was held. The Nepali Congress Party led by B.P. Koirala gained power. But in 1960, after constant friction between the king and cabinet, Tribhuvan's son, King Mahendra, dissolved parliament. In 1962 a new constitution, which banned all political parties and gave absolute power to the king, was adopted.

In 1979 discontent at rampant government corruption led to riots by the people. The king held a national referendum to decide whether to have a multiparty system or continue with the 1962 constitution. The king won by a narrow majority. Yet, poverty and corruption persisted.

In 1990, after a series of bloody riots between leftist demonstrators and the police, in which hundreds of citizens were killed, King Birendra gave up most of his power to a democratically elected, multiparty parliament.

MAOIST REBELS

A Maoist guerrilla movement began in Nepal's countryside in 1996. The aim of the movement is to overthrow the current government and set up a communist government in Nepal based on the ideals of China's Communist Revolution. The Maoist guerrillas spread throughout the nation and gained strength in the late 1990s. The Maoist rebels have attacked government property, killing hundreds of civilians in the process. The rebels have also had armed confrontations with Nepal's police. In July 2001, the Maoist rebels agreed to a ceasefire proposed by the government. In November 2001, talks between the rebels and the government failed, leading to a relaunch of attacks by the rebels.

ROYAL TRAGEDY

In June 2001, King Birendra, the queen, and most of the royal family were killed during a bloody shooting in the royal palace. The official account maintains that Crown Prince Dipendra, King Birendra's son, shot most of the royal family, before fatally wounding himself, after an argument with his parents over his choice of bride. Gyanendra, King Birendra's brother, was crowned king three days after the shootings.

GOVERNMENT

AFTER A BRIEF moment of democracy—from 1959 to 1960—the monarchy reasserted control. In 1990, after forceful "people power" demonstrations by mostly leftist protesters, King Birendra gave up his almost absolute power in favor of a parliamentary democracy.

The Nepali Congress Party won the 1991 parliamentary elections. Since then it has alternated in power with the Nepal Communist Party. A lack of stability and the general corruption of all Nepalese political parties, however, have led to widespread dissatisfaction among the people. In 1996 an armed Maoist guerrilla movement was formed in western Nepal; it spread rapidly throughout the country. The mysterious murder of almost the entire royal family in 2001 has deepened doubts about Nepal's future.

ADMINISTRATIVE ORGANIZATION

Nepal has a bicameral parliament. The House of Representatives has 205 members elected to a five-year term. The upper house is called the National Council. It has 60 members; 35 members are chosen by the House of Representatives, 10 by the king, and 15 by a special electoral college.

The prime minister, chosen by the parliament's majority party, holds executive power. However, the choice of prime minister and the members of his cabinet must be approved by the king. The system of government is similar to that in England, except that the Nepalese king holds more power than the English monarch.

Nepal is divided into 14 *anchal* ("AHN-chel"), or zones. Each *anchal* is divided into *jilla* ("JILL-lah"), or districts. There are 75 *jilla*, each with a legislative assembly. Each district is divided into villages. Each village has a village assembly. Every Nepalese citizen aged 18 or above can vote in elections for village, district, and national assemblies.

"Nepal is like a yam between two boulders [China and India]."

—*Prithvi Narayan Shah*

Opposite: **The Nepalese government building—Singha Durbar—was an old Rana palace.**

Civil servants in Nepal wear the *dara-sarwal* ("dah-rah SERH-wahl"), the traditional male suit, beneath a western-style jacket.

PEOPLE POWER

Except for B.P. Koirala, who was democratically elected prime minister in 1959, Nepal has always been governed by a strong figure who came to power either by birthright or force, or both. The king *was* the government. Everyone was ultimately answerable to the king; the king answered only to himself.

Momentum for change came in the 1980s with the rise of a young, educated class. Economic growth was poor, opportunities for the educated were limited, and the foreign aid pouring into the country had little effect on their lives. Knowledge of international affairs meant the Nepalese were aware of "people power" movements in the Philippines and Eastern Europe. These events inspired them to demand change in Nepal.

Demonstrations broke out in 1990. On April 3 the army fired into a crowd of demonstrators near the royal palace killing 45 people. This tragic event led King Birendra to start the change to democracy. In 1991 the Nepali Congress Party won the first free election. The party's leader, G.P. Koirala—B.P. Koirala's brother—became prime minister.

Since then, power has alternated between the Nepali Congress Party, a coalition of Communist parties, and the right-wing Rastriya Prajanatantra Party. Political bickering and power grabs, however, have prevented stability or progress in the nation.

NO STABILITY IN SIGHT

The Nepalese have grown disillusioned with democracy as political promises have turned out empty. In 1996 a Maoist rebellion developed in western Nepal, based on the beliefs of

With democracy come political rallies. Here, members of the Marxist-Leninist party parade in the street.

China's Mao Zedong. This Maoist movement has spread to the whole country. It has also grown increasingly violent. Thousands have died, many of them members of Nepal's police force. In 2001 the government entered into the first face-to-face talks with the Maoists, but there has been no progress in reaching a settlement.

Nepal's political situation was further aggravated on June 1, 2001, after the killing of almost the entire royal family. Birendra's only surviving brother, Gyanendra, was crowned king amid much public outrage, as many Nepalese doubted the official explanation of the killings, which pointed to Crown Prince Dipendra as the sole culprit. King Gyanendra has vowed to investigate the killings and continue talks with the Maoists.

ECONOMY

BY ANY MEASURE, Nepal is one of the poorest and most underdeveloped countries in the world. The per capita income is only about USD 200 a year. This figure ranks Nepal as one of the five poorest countries in the world.

Nepal's harsh geography, the lack of almost any natural resources, a high population growth rate, and political instability make improving the economic situation very difficult.

There is a huge income distribution gap. The lowest 10 percent of households receives only 3.2 percent of the national income. The top 10 percent receives 30 percent. Forty-two percent of the population lives below the poverty line.

Over 80 percent of the labor force relies on agriculture. Large areas of the Middle Hills suffer from a food deficit, which means that farmers cannot produce enough to feed their families. The government must rely on food aid and imports to feed the population. Many farmers in the Middle Hills are forced to seek seasonal work in the lowlands and in India.

Agriculture accounts for 41 percent of the gross domestic product (GDP). Industry, mainly carpets and textiles, accounts for 22 percent. The service sector, mainly tourism, contributes 37 percent.

Economists estimate Nepal needs an annual growth rate of 6 percent to achieve any real economic progress. In the early 1990s, Nepal actually achieved this growth figure, which has since dropped to slightly over 3 percent.

Opposite: **Nepalese women plant rice. Farm work is always done collectively by members of the community.**

Below: **All goods are transported through hills on the rugged backs of porters. Development comes slowly due to the lack of roads, electricity, and other industrial necessities.**

A group of Nepalese women plant rice near the town of Pokhara. Rice is the staple food in Nepal.

AGRICULTURE

In Nepal agriculture depends on altitude, because changes in altitude affect the climate. Rice, for example, can only be grown up to about 6,500 feet (1,980 m). Corn, wheat, and millet can be grown higher, up to about 9,000 feet (2,743 m). In the highest altitudes, up to about 14,000 feet (4,267 m), people depend on barley, buckwheat, and potatoes.

Agriculture depends on water, too. Irrigation is usually necessary to grow rice. The higher the altitude, the fewer the sources of water, thus growing rice becomes more difficult. Below 2,100 feet (640 m), in the *terai*, on the other hand, it is often possible to grow two crops of rice a year.

Nepal's principal crops are rice, wheat, corn, millet, buckwheat, barley, potatoes, sugarcane, lentils, and jute. The fertile *terai* produces a sizable surplus, but it is still not enough to feed the entire population. In addition, it is better for Nepal's economy to accept food aid and sell the surplus.

INDUSTRY

Until the mid-1980s, Nepal's leading export was jute, a fiber spun from the jute plant and used to weave burlap bags. In the late 1980s Nepal's carpet industry gave Nepal its first industrial boom.

The carpet industry has its roots in the Tibetan refugee community. Swiss relief workers working with Tibetan refugees discovered three individuals who knew traditional designs and carpet-making techniques and worked with them to develop a carpet industry as a way for the refugees to earn money.

The carpets became popular in Europe, particularly in Germany. Soon, the Tibetans were not the only ones making carpets; factories using Nepalese workers sprang up all over the Kathmandu Valley.

The boom subsided when consumers discovered that carpet production required a great deal of child labor and caused pollution. The industry tried to clean up its labor and environmental practices, but problems still remain and the carpet industry has been badly affected.

In the late 1990s, pashmina shawls woven in Nepal became popular around the world. Pashmina is the cashmere-like hair of mountain goats. Export of pashminas nearly doubled from the year 2000 to 2001.

Tourists in the Durbar Square of Kathmandu. Tourism is Nepal's greatest source of revenue.

TOURISM

Nepal's largest service industry by far is tourism. The country is a tourist's dream, blessed with stunning natural beauty and beautiful monuments. However, political instability since 1990 and the recent royal tragedy have had a negative impact on tourism.

Unfortunately, an estimated 60 percent of the foreign currency earned from tourism leaves Nepal. It pays for imported goods to support tourism; little money actually goes into the pockets of the people.

Trekking, a popular tourist activity, makes heavy demands on Nepal's ecosystem. For instance, firewood needed to cook meals and heat hot water for trekkers is obtained by cutting down trees.

There is also a movement for more responsible tourism. Projects like the Annapurna Conservation Area collect fees from visitors and work with local communities in developmental programs.

TRADE

About 50 percent of Nepal's trade is with India. The trade balance is skewed heavily in India's favor. The situation is the same with its other trading partners—the amount of goods Nepal imports from these countries is three times more than the amount of goods it is able to export to them.

DEVELOPMENT AID

Some cynical critics maintain that foreign aid, not tourism, is Nepal's leading industry. In 1998, 70 percent of Nepal's development budget came from foreign sources. Development aid, in the form of grants and loans, accounted for 10 percent of the GDP that year.

Aid from foreign governments often funds projects to build road networks, water and electrical systems, and other infrastructure. Much of the aid given to Nepal goes out of the country to pay foreign contractors hired to carry out the projects. Japan, India, the United States, and many European countries are major donors to Nepal.

Many development projects are aimed at improving Nepal's social conditions. The women here are digging trenches to lay pipes for the supply of water to their village.

International bodies, such as the United Nations, the World Bank, and the Asian Development Bank, also fund big projects in Nepal. These projects often are criticized for ignoring the concerns of the local people.

Nongovernmental organizations (NGOs), such as CARE, Save the Children, and Oxfam International, are also active in Nepal. Their projects are often carried out on a smaller scale and involve mostly social development work.

35

ENVIRONMENT

THE SOARING HIMALAYAN MOUNTAINS seem to embody strength and power; but like the rest of Nepal's landscape, the Himalayas are extremely fragile and vulnerable to deforestation.

The Nepalese rely on trees for about 80 percent of their energy needs. Most people cook and heat using only firewood. As Nepal's population is rapidly increasing, more trees need to be cut to meet rising energy needs. Hillsides devoid of trees erode rapidly and, in the process, lose their productive soil. Without this rich soil, fields become barren and vital crops will not thrive.

The rising number of people migrating to the Kathmandu Valley from the countryside has resulted in an increase in motor vehicles in the capital city. Air pollution levels in Nepal are now among the highest in the world.

Nepal's rich and diverse wildlife is also increasingly being threatened. Recent conservation efforts to save the Bengal tiger, the Asian one-horned rhinoceros, the gharial crocodile, the Ganges freshwater dolphin, and the snow leopard have met with some success, but most of these species continue to be threatened with extinction. In addition, plants that have been used as herbal remedies for centuries are taken from the people of the hills to meet the strong demand for them in other countries. Most of these plants are smuggled to India.

Hundreds of streams and rivers flowing down Nepal's mountains and hills give the country the potential to generate 83 million megawatts of electricity, enough power to supply the whole of Great Britain. However, Nepal's hostile geography, coupled with the country's scarce economic resources, makes this great potential difficult to develop.

Above: **Nepal's rivers are a potential source of energy. They are also an important medium of transportation.**

Opposite: **A yellow mustard field flourishes at an altitude of 23,000 feet (7,000 m).**

DEFORESTATION

In the 1950s the government nationalized and centralized the management of all of Nepal's forests. Prior to this, each village had managed its own forest area. The villagers made sure to conserve and nurture the land that provided them with their only source of food. Once the forests were nationalized, developers exploited the forests for financial profit.

Rich forests full of valuable trees once covered Nepal's *terai*. Migration to the *terai* has resulted in forests being cleared. Tree roots absorb runoff from the monsoon rains, keeping the fields from flooding. Trees also slow down the flow of rainwater by blocking the path of runoff. As the fields become barren, runoff increases, washing away the productive topsoil from fields. These floods also kill livestock and dozens of people annually.

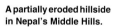

A partially eroded hillside in Nepal's Middle Hills.

FIREWOOD ALTERNATIVES

Starting in the late 1980s and throughout the 1990s, Nepal's government reversed its former policy by giving control of the forests back to the local people. Foreign aid donors sponsored projects to create tree nurseries. "Community forests" are now a part of most villages again.

Deforestation, nevertheless, remains a serious problem, as most Nepalese still rely on trees for firewood (*above*), fodder for livestock, and building materials. As Nepal's population continues to increase at a rate of 3 percent a year, forest resources will continue to decrease.

Since most firewood is burned as cooking fuel, efforts are being made to find more efficient ways to use it. Most food is cooked over an open fire or a stove with no chimney called a *chulo* ("CHEW-low"). A stove with a chimney, which allows firewood to burn for a longer time, has been developed, but the Nepalese complain that it does not emit enough light to brighten their homes. Also, the wood smoke they need to keep away insects escapes through the chimney.

Another alternative is to use bio-gas from manure and agricultural waste to power gas stoves and lights. However, these appliances are too expensive for the average farmer to afford and consume a valuable source of fertilizer the farmers need for their crops.

WILDLIFE CONSERVATION

Nepal's abundant and exotic wildlife is worth preserving not only because of its importance to the environment, but also because of its great economic potential—every year thousands of tourists come to Nepal to see the country's amazing wildlife.

The Nepali government created wildlife preserves long before their benefits were recognized and often in the face of local opposition. Nepal's most famous park, Chitwan, grew out of a royal hunting preserve.

Although many animals continue to face extinction, valuable breeding projects have at least stabilized endangered populations. There are now about 110 Bengal tigers and 500 Asian one-horned rhinoceros, a quarter of their worldwide population, in Chitwan.

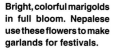

Bright, colorful marigolds in full bloom. Nepalese use these flowers to make garlands for festivals.

Royal Chitwan National Park has grown into Nepal's second most popular tourist destination (Kathmandu is the first) thanks to the cooperation of the local people. At first, there were only a few exclusive hotels near the park that catered to wealthy tourists. Revenue from these hotels had little effect on the lives of the local people, as most of the money earned was used to pay for the imported goods needed by the tourists.

At night, wildlife from the park used to cross the river surrounding the preserve and destroy farmers' crops. As the number of tourists on a low budget increased, inexpensive hotels owned and run by Nepalese sprung up around the edges of the park. Since these hotels employed local people, the community's economy improved. There was also more money generated to pay for the upkeep of the park; thus, fences were built around the park to keep the animals inside.

An Asian one-horned rhinoceros and her young in Chitwan National Park.

A three-wheeled *tempo* taxi in Kathmandu.

INCENTIVES FOR NATIONAL PARKS Some local and international incentives have given Chitwan and the local community a boost. In 1995 the Buffer Zone Act set aside half the park fees for local use, which includes relocation of communities living within the park's boundaries. The King Mahendra Trust for Nature Conservation has worked with villagers to set up tours of local community forests. The United Nations Development Program also works with local communities. There are proposals to further develop the buffer zone around the park and link it with animal migration routes to parks in India.

AIR POLLUTION

In the 1980s large numbers of Nepalese from the countryside migrated to the Kathmandu Valley to work in the carpet and garment industries. The amount of traffic in the valley grew with the population. The import of vehicles to support foreign aid programs also increased traffic.

A United Nations report states that the air quality in Kathmandu is probably the worst in the world. The valley's bowl-like shape holds in exhaust pollutants.

Tiny three-wheeled vehicles called *tempo* ("TEM-po") are the worst polluters. To cut down pollution, an electric *tempo* has been introduced.

An estimated 95 percent of the vehicles in Kathmandu exceed world emission standards. The government passed a ban on all vehicles over 20 years old, to be enforced starting in 2001. However, in May 2001 the government postponed the ban and has yet to set a new date.

WATER PROBLEMS

The carpet boom of the 1980s certainly helped the Nepali economy, but the environmental damage was also great. There were few environmental regulations in place at the time, and most people did not know how to enforce them. Carpet factories simply dumped waste directly into the valley's rivers or into pits dug at the factories. As a consequence, Kathmandu's rivers are horribly polluted.

Fifty percent of the water in Kathmandu's water system is of "unsatisfactory" quality according to international standards. Poor quality pipes are mostly to blame. By some estimates, 50 percent of the water leaks out from the pipes as pollutants and sewage leak in. People must boil and filter their water. In the dry season, long lines of people wait for hours near public taps for only a few minutes of water flow a day.

Women line up by a public tap to fill their containers with water.

MELTING GLACIERS

Nepal has not escaped the consequences of global warming. According to a report by the Worldwatch Institute, the ice in Himalayan glaciers is expected to shrink by 20 percent by the year 2035.

A 598,000-square-yard (715,000-square-m) lake of melted ice now sits behind a natural dam at Imja Glacier in the Everest region. The water is expected to burst out sometime within the next five years. In 1985 a similar glacial lake burst, hurtling water for 56 miles (90 km) downstream, washing away fields, homes, livestock, and people.

43

NEPALESE

THERE ARE DOZENS of distinct ethnic groups in Nepal. Although these groups have been living together for hundreds of years, there has been little blending or mixing. But there has always been a great deal of tolerance among the groups.

In Nepal, neighbors may worship different gods and speak different languages, but nobody thinks there is anything strange about that. Nepalese like to compare the different ways they live, and the unique customs of the various ethnic groups are a favorite topic of conversation.

Nepal is a very hierarchical society, influenced by the caste system that originated in the dominant religion, Hinduism, and was codified by the early Malla kings.

The hill groups are outside the caste system, but they have a class system of their own . Each group is divided into clans. These clans, in turn, are further subdivided into extended families.

Nepal's population can be divided into four main groups: the Hindu caste groups, the hill tribes, the Bhotes, and the Newar.

Opposite: **A Nepalese girl from Bhaktapur carries her younger brother.**

Below: **The lines on this man's face tell the story of the difficult life in the mountains of Nepal. Yet hill tribe people remain very friendly and hospitable.**

Only people born into the Brahmin caste are allowed to become Hindu priests and carry out the many rites and rituals for the gods.

HINDU CASTE GROUPS

The people of the Hindu caste groups migrated to Nepal between the 12th and 15th centuries, when they were driven from their homes in India by Muslim invaders. They were originally of Aryan stock and have Caucasian features, but with a darker complexion. They brought with them their

Indo-Aryan language, which evolved into Nepali, Nepal's national language.

The Hindu religion has a strict hierarchy known as the caste system. There are four main groups within the caste system: Brahmins ("BRAH-mins"), Chhetris ("CHE-trees"), Vaisyas ("VIE-siahs"), and Sudras ("SOO-drahs"). Hindus believe that humans sprang from the body of Brahma, the god and creator of everything. Brahmins came from Brahma's head and mouth, Chhetris from his arms, Vaisyas from his thighs, and Sudras from his feet.

A group of Chhetri children in western Nepal. These children belong to the warrior caste. Traditionally, they are not allowed to mix with children of lower castes.

At the top of the caste system are the Brahmins, the priestly caste. They are forbidden by tradition to drink alcohol and eat certain foods like onions, tomatoes, and eggs. A Brahmin must officiate at religious events, and they are the only group allowed to read the Hindu religious texts.

Below the Brahmins are the Chhetris, the warrior caste. Nepal's king is a Chhetri of the Thakuri subcaste. Traditionally, many of Nepal's army officers were Chhetri, and even today many Chhetris join the military.

Only Brahmins and Chhetris have the right to wear the *janai* ("jyah-NIGH"), the sacred thread draped across the chest that is the symbol of high status.

Below the Brahmins and Chhetris are the Vaisyas, the caste of tradesmen and artisans. Below them, at the bottom of the caste system, are the Sudras, or the occupational caste.

OCCUPATIONAL CASTES

At the lower end of the Hindu hierarchy are the occupational castes. People of these castes take their names from the traditional jobs they perform. Some examples are: Kami ("KAH-mee"), or blacksmiths; Damai ("dah-MY"), or tailors and musicians; and Sarki ("SERH-kee"), or cobblers.

The Sudras are traditionally looked down on by the rest of Nepalese society. Many of them have to endure discrimination all their lives, even from the casteless hill tribes. Most Nepalese will not allow people from the occupational castes inside their homes.

Today, many Sudras have abandoned their traditional occupations and work as porters or day laborers. Ready-made clothes, shoes, and tools have made most of their traditional occupations unnecessary. The Sudras, however, remain at the bottom of the social and economic ladder in Nepal.

A hardworking tailor in a village. Although vital to the community, jobs like these are considered the lowest form of work, and people who do these jobs are looked down on. This attitude is, however, slowly changing.

A Magar woman wearing jewelry common to the hill tribe women of Nepal. The gold nose pin is called the *phuli* ("FOO-lee").

HILL PEOPLES

The ancestors of Nepal's many hill groups crossed the high mountain passes from Tibet or followed the mountain trails from Burma. The hill peoples have Mongoloid features and speak their own languages.

The hill groups cluster in villages at altitudes of 6,000 to 9,000 feet (1,829 to 2,743 m). Young men from these groups predominate in the famous Gurkha soldier units. Although these groups are casteless, they are subdivided into clans of different status. The Gurung, for example, have four upper clans and 16 lower ones.

Hill peoples practice a religion that is often a combination of Buddhism and Hinduism and sometimes animism. In general, they are less conservative than caste Hindus and are more open in their relationships. Teenage boys and girls will openly flirt and court each other, behavior that is almost never seen among their Hindu caste neighbors.

Most hill peoples work as farmers, but they also keep large herds of goats and sheep. They sell the wool and meat from their herds in the market. Every year some members of every family must take the family's sheep and goats to high pastures of 12,000 to 14,000 feet (3,658 to 4,267 m), where it is easy to obtain good fodder for their herds.

Young men of the Rai and Limbu groups of eastern Nepal wear their best for an annual festival. The hat they wear, the *topi* ("TOH-pee"), is the national hat of Nepal.

RAI AND LIMBU Also known as Kirati, these two peoples live throughout the eastern hills of Nepal extending across the border into India. The men of these groups often carry a large *khukuri* ("KHOO-koo-ree"), the traditional Nepali knife with a curved blade, tucked into a long cloth wrapped around the waist.

The Kirati are famous for the beautiful stone masonry of their farm terraces. They also build *chautara* ("CHOW-tah-rah"), stone resting platforms topped by large, shady pipal trees, on the trail outside villages as memorials to the dead.

TAMANG Tamang are the largest of the hill groups. They are also the most independent, retaining their own language and Buddhist religion even as other groups fall under increasing Nepali and Hindu influence. In Tibetan, *tamang* means "horse trader."

Tamang live in the high hills to the north, east, and west of Kathmandu. They often come to the city to work as porters and day laborers.

The preferred marriage partner is one's cross-cousin. For a man, this is his father's sister's daughter or his mother's brother's daughter.

GURUNG Gurung live in the hills around Pokhara and east toward Gorkha. They, and the Magar, formed the bulk of Prithvi Narayan Shah's army when he conquered the Kathmandu Valley.

The military is still the main profession of the Gurung. Most families have at least one member serving in India or in the British army. Retired soldiers and their pensions are funding growth in Pokhara and other traditional Gurung hill areas.

Those remaining at home turn to farming and goat rearing. From April to September, a member of the family will take the sheep, cows, and water buffalo to high pastures, some above 14,000 feet (4,267 m).

These two Gurung teenagers take a break from carrying their load of goat- and sheepskins. They will sell these skins in Kathmandu after a five-day walk from their village.

MAGAR Like the Gurung, the Magar also live in central and western Nepal. In the 17th century, they had a very strong kingdom in what is now Palpa, and Prithvi Narayan Shah also depended heavily on them for his armies. Even today, the Magar send the greatest number of men to the military.

As the southernmost of the hill groups, the Magar have had the longest contact with caste Hindus from India. Consequently, the Magar are the most heavily Hindu-influenced of the hill peoples.

Southern Magar have arranged marriages. The boy's parents send a representative with a bottle of rice beer to the girl's parents. If the beer is accepted, so is the proposal.

Sherpa women are very independent and hold more power in their homes than women in Hindu caste homes.

SHERPAS Saying "Sherpa" has become the equivalent of saying "mountain guide" to most tourists, but the term should only be used for a group living mainly in the high valleys of the Everest region.

Born at an altitude of more than 12,000 feet (3,658 m), at the base of the highest mountains in the world, Sherpas are naturally acclimatized to high-altitude mountain climbing.

Sherpas settled in the Everest area about 300 years ago after crossing over from Tibet. They were well-known as traders long before they earned their fame as mountain porters and guides.

BHOTES

Across Nepal's north, in high valleys of over 9,000 feet (2,743 m), are groups of people called Bhotiya or Bhotes. The Bhote culture is essentially Tibetan (*Bho* is another name for Tibet).

Isolated by the Himalayan mountains, they live as farmers, sheep and yak herders, and lately as hoteliers to the tourist trade. They are also known as traders, traveling far beyond Nepal's borders. Most famous are the Manangi from the Manang valley, who received special trading rights from two previous Nepali kings.

MUSLIMS

Small communities of Muslim traders arrived in Kathmandu from Kashmir in the 15th century and again in the 18th century at the invitation of Nepal's king.

After the Indian Mutiny of 1857—a revolt led by Indian soldiers against British rule—some Muslim refugees fleeing India settled in Nepal. The British eventually defeated the Indian soldiers after a bloody retaliation with some help from Nepalese forces. For its contribution in helping the British put down the mutiny, Nepal received land that had belonged to the Nawab of Oudh, one of the mutiny's leaders. This area, including Nepalganj in the west, is the center of Islamic culture in Nepal today.

Unlike in India, Nepal's Hindu and Islamic cultures have always coexisted peacefully.

A Bhote family dressed in all their finery. In the hills, where the infant mortality rate is high, families have many children.

Newar women of the farmer caste wear their distinctive costume of a black sari with a red border along the hem.

NEWAR

The Newar are the indigenous inhabitants of the Kathmandu Valley, where they have been living for the past 1,500 years. Their language originated from a mixture of Tibeto-Burmese and Sanskrit. The Newar language is one of the most complex languages in the world.

There are Newar communities in many of Nepal's larger towns. Almost all Newar work as merchants and shopkeepers. It was the Newar who built most of the temples and crafted most of the sculptures Kathmandu is famous for.

The Newar have a highly structured caste system, which the Malla kings dictated over 600 years ago. As the Kathmandu Valley modernizes, old caste restrictions on occupation are slowly fading. However, the social restrictions of the caste system are still largely observed. Newar very rarely marry outside their caste, and those who do risk being cut off from their community by their family and friends.

REMOTE GROUPS

There are several ethnic groups in Nepal that do not fit into any of the major groups:

THARU (*above*) are the indigenous people of the *terai*. Their natural immunity to malaria allowed them to survive in the jungle for centuries before modern insecticides opened the *terai* to other Nepalese.

Living as marginal farmers in settlements scattered throughout the thick jungle, the Tharu are generally shy and have little experience with money. This has made them an easy target for ruthless moneylenders, who seize the Tharu's best land when they are unable to repay their debts.

The Tharu remain one of the poorest and most exploited groups in Nepal.

CHEPANG are a group living in the most remote areas of the southern-middle hills of central Nepal. Shy around outsiders, they lived until recently as hunter-gatherers, woodcutters, and sometimes farmers.

They were severely exploited by their better-educated, more aggressive caste Hindu neighbors. The government has started several programs to help them.

LIFESTYLE

THERE ARE SO MANY DIFFERENT CULTURES in Nepal that the way people think and do things can vary tremendously from one house to the next. Neighbors may speak a different language, worship different gods, even celebrate a different day as New Year's Day. To a Nepalese, this is natural and everyone is extremely tolerant of the different traditions people hold.

Each cultural group in Nepal has a hierarchical structure. There are divisions and rankings within a family, an extended family, an ethnic group, and society as a whole. This system, too, is something Nepalese have grown accustomed to.

The caste system has been outlawed by the government but still plays a large role in everyday life. Attitudes are slowly changing, particularly in urban areas, and low-caste people do not carry the stigma they once did. The government is trying to widen opportunities for everyone.

Names in Nepal say more about the person than Western names do. Names indicate one's caste or group, one's profession, and even where one is from.

If one met Mr. Khatiwanda, one would know from his name that he is a Brahmin and probably from western Nepal. Mr. Pokhrel is a Brahmin, too, but from the east. Mr. Sakya is a Newar, and works as a silversmith or goldsmith. As there are many rules regarding interaction between castes, knowing people's names settles the question of whether one can accept the rice they cook or visit their home. These customs are no longer as widely practiced as they were before.

Opposite: **Women sell flower garlands to be used as offerings in Hindu rituals.**

Below: **Leaves and vines are woven tightly together to form a waterproof roof. The leaves also trap heat to keep the house warm on cold nights.**

It is common to find extended families of several generations living together in a single household in Nepal. The extended family includes grandparents, uncles, aunts, and cousins.

FAMILY STRUCTURE

When Nepalese say "my family," they are speaking of a much larger family unit than most Westerners have. Cousins are called "brothers and sisters," a mother's oldest sister is called "oldest mother," a father's youngest brother is "youngest father," and so on.

Several generations commonly live under the same roof. Sons customarily stay in the home after marriage, bringing their wife to live with them and raising their children in their family homes.

The money earned by every member of the family goes into a treasury that is controlled by the head of the household, usually the oldest male. He has the final say in all important family decisions, such as children's education, jobs, and marriage partners.

Bhote women have a stronger position at home than most other Nepalese woman. As Bhote men are away from home trading most of the time, the women make most of the household decisions.

GROWING UP

Name-giving is the first important milestone for an infant in a Hindu home. Customs vary from group to group, but the name is determined by an astrologer based on the exact time of birth.

Almost all groups have a rice-feeding ceremony called *pausni* ("PAHS-nee") when a baby is about six months old. Many guests are invited for this ceremony, and the parents will hold a big feast. Guests often give the infant money to wish him or her future prosperity.

During a Newar *pausni,* several objects may be placed in front of the baby—dirt, unhusked rice, a brick, toys, a pen, or a hook. The parents and priest predict the child's future talents or occupation based on which object the infant reaches for first.

At about the age of 5, male Brahmins and Chhetris have their head shaved except for a small tuft of hair toward the back of the head called a *tupi* ("TOO-pee"). The *tupi* indicates that the boy is a Hindu.

Even among the poorest families, parents cherish and often indulge their children.

PUBERTY

When approaching puberty, male Brahmins and Chhetris receive a *janai,* a sacred thread made up of three loops of cotton twine, worn over the right shoulder and under the left arm. The *janai* is a sign of high caste and is changed once a year, during the full moon of July or August. After completing this ceremony, the boy is allowed to eat with other adult men.

At the age of 12, boys have their heads shaved, are bathed, dressed in saffron robes, given alms bowls, and sent off begging, as the Buddha did thousands of years ago. However, the boys are sent only to the homes of their relatives and neighbors and return home on the same day.

Before they reach puberty, Newar girls go through their first marriage—to a *bel* ("bale"), a wood apple. The *bel* represents the god Subarna Kumar. Since the full marriage rites can only be performed once, their subsequent marriage is of secondary importance and they are free to divorce and remarry.

Newar boys celebrate the onset of puberty with the Bratabhanda ceremony. On this day, the boys will follow in the footsteps of the Buddha and go "begging" to the homes of their neighbors and relatives.

In Hindu and Newar homes, a daughter reaching puberty is no cause for celebration. During her first menstruation, she is locked in a room for 14 days. Considered unclean, she is forbidden to see or be seen by the men of the house or to touch any food but her own. Sometimes even the women of her own house avoid her touch.

60

MARRIAGE

Almost all marriages in Nepal are between members of the same caste or ethnic group. Intercaste marriages are extremely rare, as both husband and wife will be cut off from their respective families.

Hindu and Newar marriages are usually arranged. A relative of either the bride or groom acts as a go-between, carrying photos of the boy and girl and persuading both sets of parents. Sometimes the couple is allowed to meet, but only if accompanied by many chaperones.

There are three types of marriages among the hill groups: arranged marriages, free courtship, or "kidnapping." Once the boy "kidnaps" the girl of his choice, he has three days to convince her to marry him. If she refuses, he must release her. Wedding customs vary widely from group to group.

Although it is illegal, polygamy, or having more than one spouse at any one time, still occurs in Nepal. As Islam allows it, Muslims are exempted from this law. The most common reason for taking another wife is the inability of the first wife to bear a son. All the wives may live together or separately.

Because the men are often away on trading trips, a Bhote woman may marry several brothers at the same time. All children, however, are considered to be the eldest brother's children.

A Hindu wedding in Nepal. The bride sits with her head covered while Brahmin priests pray for the gods' blessing. The groom is at the back.

DOMESTIC ARCHITECTURE

Houses in the Himalayas are usually built stacked on top of each other and close together in order to keep in the heat and keep out the cold.

Housing style in Nepal varies according to ethnic group and regional climate. Many people in the *terai* build their homes on stilts and keep their animals below the house. Living above the ground gives them some protection from snakes, animals, and mosquitoes. It is also much cooler and breezier. Every house has a separate compound.

Higher up in the hills, where there are fewer snakes and winters are colder, houses are more solid, with thick stone walls and thatched or slate-tile roofs. Windows are small, without glass panes. There is no chimney for the fire. The creosote, a strong-smelling, oily liquid in wood smoke, coats the ceiling wood and protects it from bugs. Houses are built close together, and two or three homes may share a compound.

In the high Himalayan region, people live on the second floor, like people in the *terai,* but they do it as protection from the cold. Their homes often share a wall with a neighbor's, as homes built together stand a better chance of keeping the cold out. Animals live beneath the house, and their body heat helps to warm the rooms above. The houses are built of stone and wood, with wooden roof shingles weighed down by heavy stones.

THE HEARTH

Each ethnic group places special importance on the hearth and cooking area. A non-Brahmin should never enter the cooking area in a Brahmin house. To do so would pollute the area, and a religious "cleansing" ceremony would have to be performed.

A Brahmin male must take off his clothes and wrap a length of white cloth called a *dhoti* ("DHOH-tee") around himself before he steps into the hearth area to eat.

In the Middle Hills and Himalayas, though, a guest will immediately be given the best seat by the hearth—on the right side, near the back wall of the hearth.

Most social activity in Nepal takes place around the fire—usually an open pit with an iron tripod where pots are placed. Nepalese people have great respect for the hearth, and they are careful not to throw anything that could be considered "unclean" into it.

In the northern hills the hearth is the center of the house. Guests are asked to sit by the fire as soon as they arrive.

In the villages, many household chores take place outside the home. It is common to do the laundry at the nearest spring or river.

A TYPICAL DAY IN THE VILLAGE

Work in the village begins before the roosters crow. There is wood to be gathered, fodder to be cut, and water to be fetched. Water may come from a nearby well or from a stream or tap over an hour's walk away. As the forests disappear, water is quickly disappearing too, and people have to walk farther and farther for both fuel and water.

The fire is lit and cooking starts as soon as the household stirs. There may be tea with sugar for breakfast, but probably not every morning. Most people eat *derdho* ("DAIR-dhoh")—a mixture of millet, corn, and wheat flour boiled into a thick paste. To go with this, there may be lentil soup and some vegetable curry (potato is most common), or just vegetables with broth. If the family cow or water buffalo has a calf, there may be milk or yogurt.

After breakfast, some children go to school, while others help out in the fields or at home. School starts at 10 A.M.

Whether it is farm work, grazing cattle, or getting wood or water, everything is done by hand and carried on a person's back. After school, children may play or join their parents at work.

Villagers use the sun, not watches or clocks, to tell time. As the sun begins to set, everyone gathers around the fire. Light may come from a tiny kerosene lamp or just from the fire. After eating dinner (probably *derdho* again), the family gathers to talk until everyone goes to sleep.

A TYPICAL DAY IN TOWN

Nepalese living in towns are also early risers. Nothing tastes better than a steaming glass of Nepali milk tea on a cold morning. Water may be available in the house or have to be fetched from a nearby tap. The mother starts work right away because it can take two hours to cook on her single-burner kerosene stove. She prepares a meal of rice, lentil soup, vegetable curry, and maybe milk or yogurt. Meanwhile, the children get ready for school.

The father then goes to his shop or office, and the mother begins her housework. If the parents can afford it, they send their children to private English schools. The school "bus" may be anything from a rickshaw to a rickety old van.

The mother washes the dishes and clothes at the nearest communal tap and then goes to the market to buy vegetables and other food items for the day, since there is no refrigerator to store a week's groceries. After school, the children play, study, or maybe go see the new Indian movie in town—the cheap seats cost only about USD 5 cents.

These schoolchildren happily look forward to playing with their friends after the ride home in a bicycle rickshaw.

The father finishes his work at 5 P.M. and makes his way home slowly. He talks to friends, maybe over a cup of tea or local liquor, and stops at the newsstand to browse through the latest books and magazines. When he comes home, he checks his children's homework. In each room candles are always handy, in case there is a blackout.

The evening meal is served late, at around 8 P.M. or later, and everyone goes to bed soon afterward.

Opposite: **In the cities, some girls from middle-income families are sent to English schools. But after completing their studies, they are still expected to marry and be traditional housewives.**

Above: **Nepalese women are an unseen economic force. Women carry out many cottage industries, such as spinning and weaving.**

WOMEN IN NEPAL

Surveys show that women do over 70 percent of the work in the village, such as fetching water, fodder, and firewood, as well as hoeing, weeding, and harvesting crops. They use only basic tools. Work is still mostly done by hand and everything is carried on a person's back.

A new bride usually lives with her husband's family and must earn the respect of her in-laws through hard work at home and in the fields. Although life is difficult for Nepalese women, divorce is rare.

Women in Nepal have almost no decision-making power. Women in caste Hindu homes, in particular, are powerless. Women in Bhote families are able to hold power at home because the men are away on trading trips most of the time. Women in the hill groups are somewhere in-between.

Sons are preferred over daughters, as families must bear large expenses, including in some cases a large dowry, when a daughter marries. But as girls are needed to work in the fields, they are considered both a burden as well as a source of labor.

Although the government is trying to improve the condition of women, they are still discriminated against in many areas of Nepalese life.

A baby being vaccinated. Lines are long at Nepal's free health clinics. After walking for several hours with their babies in their arms, mothers must wait a long time for their turn.

HEALTH CARE

One out of 10 children in Nepal dies before the age of 1. Seven percent of children die before age 5, and 47 percent of children under 5 are malnourished. Nepalese families often want many children, as they do not expect all of their children to survive to adulthood.

Many of Nepal's health problems are caused by poor hygiene and sanitation facilities. Few houses have toilets. Instead, people use the nearby fields or streams. Diseases spread easily in this way. Thirty-three percent of child deaths are caused by diarrhea.

The government is trying to build a hospital in every district and a healthpost in every village committee. Still, it takes hours to travel to the healthpost and days to reach the hospital. Even after people arrive at the hospital, doctors and medicine may not be available, the result of Nepal's poor transportation and communication systems.

Whenever they fall sick, many Nepalese still rely on traditional faith healers, called *jankri* ("JAHN-kree"). The *jankri* supposedly removes the cause of the illness from the person, often by going into a trance while beating on a drum. Some *jankri* have a great deal of knowledge about medicinal plants and are able to mix herbal medicines to treat illnesses.

EDUCATION

There are very few schools in Nepal's rural areas. Students must walk, and in certain areas, it may take them up to two hours to reach school. Lessons are conducted outdoors. Classrooms are used only when necessary, as they are dark and cold because of the lack of electricity. Few textbooks are available, so students are taught to memorize their lessons.

Nepal's literacy rate is 27.5 percent. Considering the fact that in the 1950s the literacy rate was only 5 percent, the rate has improved a great deal. Still, schools, teachers, and textbooks are in short supply. Only 52 percent of men and 18 percent of women are literate.

A typical mud-brick schoolhouse in the countryside. Before class, students and teachers gather outside to sing the national anthem and do some calisthenics.

Men stack a pile of wood to prepare a funeral pyre at Pashupatinath, the most sacred temple in Nepal. Hindus believe in cremating their dead and then scattering the ashes in a river.

DEATH

Death is treated in different ways in different cultures. Hindus cremate the body by the banks of the nearest river. They then pick out a small piece of bone and throw the ashes in the river. They believe that the ashes will eventually reach the sacred waters of the Ganges River in India.

Among hill groups, the Magar and Tamang also cremate their dead, but on top of a hill. The Gurung either cremate or bury their dead. A priest decides which one it should be, based on the position of the stars at the time of the person's death.

Almost every group in Nepal has elaborate ceremonies to mark the first death anniversary. During this ceremony, the family of the dead person gives a large feast for the entire village.

Wood is scarce in the Himalayan region, and so cremation is difficult. Often the land is also too rocky for digging graves. The Bhotes, who live in this area, take the dead body to a high place, cut it up in pieces, and leave it for vultures.

COMMON COURTESIES AND ETIQUETTE

When Nepalese meet or leave each other, they join their hands in front of them in a prayer-like gesture and say *namaste* ("neh-MEHS-tay"), or sometimes *namaskar* ("neh-MEHS-kahr"). These phrases are derived from Sanskrit words and mean "I bow to the god in you."

Himalayan people drape a thin white scarf called a *khata* ("KAH-tah") around the neck of someone they want to show respect to or of someone leaving on a trip.

Nepalese seldom say *dhanyabad* ("DHAHN-yah-bahd"), meaning "thank you." People do not open a present when it is given. To avoid any chance of embarrassing anyone, they open it in private.

The feet are considered the dirtiest part of the body, while the head is considered the most sacred. A Nepalese will never step over a person. If a Nepalese touches you with his or her feet by accident, he or she will immediately reach down, touch your feet and then touch his or her own head as if to say, "I am sorry. Your feet are higher than my head."

Objects should be passed with the right hand. As the left hand is used to clean oneself after using the toilet, it is considered unclean.

RELIGION

ACCORDING TO A RECENT ESTIMATE, Nepal's population is about 86 percent Hindu, 8 percent Buddhist, and 4 percent Muslim. Two percent of the population belongs to other religions. In everyday life, though, the line between Hinduism and Buddhism is far from clear. Many Nepalese follow both religions. Hinduism, in particular, is a part of everyday life in Nepal, as it is integrated into daily routines such as shopping or going to work.

Because the Buddha is considered a form of the Hindu god Vishnu, the Buddha's teachings are well-known and have great influence even among Nepalese Hindus.

Opposite: **Hindus pay their respects in front of an image of Kala Bhairab in Kathmandu.**

Below: **A Brahmin priest gives a *tika* ("TEE-kah") to a young girl. The *tika* is a sign of blessing and a symbol of knowledge.**

Opposite: **A centuries-old sculpture of the Hindu god Vishnu. He is known as the "Preserver of the Universe."**

HINDUISM

Hinduism, the oldest living faith in the world, does not have an identifiable founder. There is no governing or regulating body, and there is no specific dogma that spells out what a Hindu should believe.

Hindus define their beliefs in a collection of philosophical writings called the Vedas, which are 1,008 hymns and revelations of saints and seers. The Vedas were first recorded over 1,000 years ago.

Hinduism embraces many beliefs, so many, in fact, that some beliefs directly contradict others. According to Hindu philosophy, there is more than one righteous path to understanding the mysteries of life. The individual's capacities, attitudes, and requirements determine his or her beliefs. To Hindus, all religions lead to the same end. Hindus may even embrace other religions without ceasing to be Hindus.

Hindus believe in reincarnation, or rebirth after death, and moving up or down a universal ladder. Their actions in this life determine their next life. If they perform bad deeds in this lifetime, they may be reborn into a lower caste, as animals, or even as insects.

If they do great good in this life, earning much *dharma* ("DHARH-mah"), or merit, then their next life will be enriched. After living thousands of lives, they may be able to go to heaven, released from the cycle of life and death at last.

To Hindus, people's condition in this world and the things that happen in their lives, are part of their *karma* ("KAHR-mah"), or destiny. Therefore, it does no good to feel anger and rebel against *karma*. *Karma* must be accepted and borne. This attitude of tolerance helps Nepalese Hindus bear their poverty, but it may also diminish their motivation for change.

HINDU GODS

One Hindu text states that there are 300 million gods, and Hindus actively worship hundreds. But three stand out: Brahma the Creator, Vishnu the Preserver, and Shiva the Destroyer. These three gods combine to become Brahman, the ultimate divinity found in everything.

A god may be called by a dozen different names and may manifest itself in several different forms. Vishnu, for example, has 10 different forms, including a lion, a dwarf, the Hindu h e r o Krishna, and even the Buddha. The Nepalese consider their king to be a manifestation of Vishnu.

Shiva, with over 108 different names, is the god most worshiped in Nepal. Known as the Destroyer, he is also called the "bright or happy one," and is honored as Lord of the Dance. He is often pictured as an ascetic, his body smeared with ashes and wrapped in a leopard skin, wandering far and wide or meditating at his home on Mount Kailash in Tibet. It is believed that the waters of the Ganges River spring from the tall pile of hair on his head.

Ganesh, Shiva's son, is one of everybody's favorite gods. His father cut off his head by mistake, and to appease his wife, swore to replace it with the first living thing he found—which turned out to be an elephant. With his elephant head and roly-poly body, Ganesh does not look like a typical immortal. Still, he is the god most people first turn to with their requests.

Durga is one of the representations of Shiva's wife, Parbati. People worship Durga for her victory over a demon during the festival of Dasain ("dah-SIGH").

Laxmi, the goddess of wealth and prosperity, is appealed to during the festival of Tihar ("TEE-hahr").

Saraswati, the goddess of wisdom and Brahman's consort, is usually portrayed riding a swan and playing a sitar, an Indian lute with a long neck.

Indra, the god of rain, is prayed to during the monsoons.

BUDDHISM

The Buddha's real name was Siddhartha Gautama. The name Buddha is an honorary title meaning "enlightened one." Siddhartha was born around 623 B.C. in Lumbini, which is now part of Nepal's *terai*. Born into a rich, perhaps noble, family, he lived a life of luxury and ease in several palaces.

Being curious about life, he made several secret trips outside the palace. Shocked by the pain, death, and suffering of the common people, he decided to renounce everything in his life, including his wife and son, to try to understand what he had seen.

For the next six years, he went through every form of deprivation as he meditated and searched for the answers to life. Finally realizing them, he became the Buddha. For the rest of his life he walked with a group of disciples, talking with anyone who listened or asked him about the meaning of life and spreading his message. He died at Bodh Ghaya in present-day India.

White prayer flags are hung outside Buddhist temples and monasteries. People believe the winds will carry their prayers to heaven.

BUDDHIST DOCTRINE All Buddhists believe that life is based on a cycle of birth, death, and rebirth. One's rebirth depends on one's *karma,* or the end result of one's actions, words, and thoughts in a lifetime. A Buddhist's goal is to break the cycle of rebirth by living a life of detachment from the desires of this world. If this is done, a person attains Nirvana, or release from the cycle of life and death. Several Buddhist schools have evolved since the Buddha's death. The Mahayana school has influenced Tibet, Nepal, and northern Asia. The Theravada school is followed in Sri Lanka

THE BUDDHA'S TEACHINGS

In Lumbini, a small temple has been built on the site where the Buddha was reputedly born, but there is little else to commemorate him. A mound and pillar built in 250 B.C. by the great Indian emperor Asoka as well as brick ruins of monasteries built about 1,000 years ago still stand amid the tall grass. Though his birthplace pays him humble homage, the Buddha's teachings have spread throughout Asia to Japan, Indochina, and even the ancient kingdoms of Indonesia.

THE FOUR NOBLE TRUTHS
- In our lives there is pain from disease, suffering, birth, and death.
- The basic cause of pain lies in our desires for material things, pleasure, and people.
- Detachment from these desires ends pain and provides an escape from the cycle of rebirth.
- The eightfold path is the way to attain this detachment.

THE EIGHTFOLD PATH
Right understanding, right thought, right speech, right action, right livelihood, right effort, right-mindedness, and right concentration.

Buddhist monks chanting. Although Buddhism first arrived in Tibet via Nepal, rites and forms of worship practiced in Nepal today draw their inspiration from Tibetan Buddhist tradition.

and Southeast Asia. One important difference between the two schools is that in Theravada philosophy believers are only concerned with their own release from the cycle. Mahayana tradition dictates that those who achieve enlightenment must "go back" and help others do the same.

A woman spins a prayer wheel. These wheels are meant to help those who are unable to read and recite the Pali scriptures of Buddhism to gain blessings.

IN DAILY LIFE

Every morning, the streets of Nepal are filled with people going to the neighborhood shrine for *puja* ("POO-jah"), or worship. People carry trays with colored powder, flower petals, grains of rice, a few sweets, and a small bell. These items are used in worship at the temple.

Many people encountered in the morning will have flower petals in their hair. This is part of *prasad* ("prah-SAHD"), the blessing received from the gods in return for worshiping them. The mark many people wear on their forehead, the *tika,* is another sign of blessing. It symbolizes the third eye of inner wisdom and vision.

Nepalese believe divinity can be found in everything: in people, in plants and animals, and even in rocks. They would rather build roads around large rocks and trees than remove them, for fear of disturbing their divinity. It is impossible for the Nepalese to separate their daily lives from their religion, as they believe their actions affect this, and the next, life.

A young girl on her way to the temple. The food is donated to the gods as an offering during *puja*.

Hindus worship the cow as their Divine Mother and also as a symbol of fertility. Cow products such as milk and yogurt and by-products such as dung and urine have special religious significance. A Hindu would never think of killing a cow or eating beef. In Nepal, cows wander loose everywhere. They have good reason to feel safe: the penalty for killing a cow, even by accident, can be up to 20 years in jail.

Both father and son are Muslims. They can be recognized by their skullcaps, which are of Middle Eastern origin.

OTHER RELIGIONS

About 4 percent of Nepal's population is Muslim. Almost all Muslims live in the western *terai*, but there is a small active community in Kathmandu. There is a very small Christian population. In certain remote areas of the Himalayas, Bon, the Tibetan religion prior to Buddhism, is still followed.

In the face of cultural and religious diversity, the Nepalese exercise great tolerance and mutual respect for the beliefs of others. They are proud that religious conflict has never been a problem in Nepal.

FOLK BELIEFS

The Nepalese have customs, superstitions, and rituals, both large and small, that cover almost all aspects of everyday life. Because of Nepal's great cultural diversity, customs that are important or offensive to one culture may mean nothing to another. Here are some customs and beliefs:

- Never blow out a light with your breath; wave something, even just your hand, to fan out the flame.
- After lighting a lamp or just switching on an electric light for the first time that day, a Nepalese will make a *namaste* gesture toward the light.
- Fresh water should be fetched every morning; water that stands overnight is considered no longer clean.
- Before serving food, Nepalese will place a little rice in the fire as an offering to the gods.
- When you see a baby for the first time, give some money (a rupee or a few coins) to guarantee his or her future prosperity.
- If a bee hovers near you, good fortune is coming.

The Nepalese travel often, and have set of beliefs about travel:

- If your feet itch, you will be traveling soon.
- Some people take a betel nut, a coin, and some rice wrapped in a cloth to ensure a safe trip.
- It is unlucky to start a journey on a Tuesday.
- It is unlucky to leave under a new moon.
- A large jug full of water on each side of the doorway ensures a safe trip.
- Try not to come back home on a Saturday.

Mothers threaten their naughty children with "a foreigner will come and eat you!" But the Nepalese already had enough strange creatures in their culture even before the arrival of foreigners:

- A *jhumi* ("JHYOO-mi") will grab you and lead you away from your house without your knowledge if you leave early in the morning without telling anyone.
- If you meet a beautiful young woman late at night, look at her feet. If they're pointed backwards, run! She's a *kichikinni* ("kee-chee-KIN-nee"), the spirit of a dead woman.
- A *mulkatta* ("mool-KAHT-tah"), a dead man's spirit, wanders around headless.
- If you wake up, but feel you can't get up, it's a *khya* ("KHEE-yah") holding you down. If a *khya* gets upset, it will tickle you to death.
- *Pret* ("preht") and *pisach* ("pee-SAHCH"), unhappy spirits, wait at crossroads and cremation sites to chase people and make them sick.

LANGUAGE

THERE ARE OVER A DOZEN LANGUAGES spoken in Nepal and each language has many dialects. In fact, dialects change with almost every ridge you cross. A Tamang from Dhading in central Nepal will have a hard time understanding a Tamang from Taplejung in the east. Because of Nepal's harsh geography, there is little interaction between groups.

Nepali is the national language, and it is used by people from different groups to speak to one another. Nepali is an Indo-European language and has many similarities to the grammar and vocabulary of Hindi, spoken in northern India. Nepali and Hindi share the same script.

NEPALI

Nepali sentence structure is very different from English construction. The usual order is subject-object-verb. There are "markers" to identify the words that are the subject, object, or indirect object. The marker for the subject is -*le*; for an indirect object the marker is -*laai*. For example:

> *Ramle Sitalaai paani diyo.*
> Ram to Sita water gave.
> (Ram gave water to Sita.)

There are two different verbs that share the function of the English verb "to be." One form is used when describing something that is so at that moment, while the other is used for a permanent state of being.

Nepali uses sounds nonexistent in English. For example, there are two "d" sounds. Nepali also uses several aspirated sounds, almost like an extra "h" added to a sound, such as "ka" and "kha." The difference in pronunciation is very difficult for a non-Nepalese to hear and pick up.

Opposite: **The Nepalese believe that if a child writes before a statue of Sarawasti, the goddess of wisdom, he or she will do well in school.**

LANGUAGE AS ETIQUETTE

The Nepali language can be very formal and polite. The words one uses will change according to whether one is talking to a friend, a shopkeeper, one's parents, or a high official. There is even a separate vocabulary for speaking to the royal family.

In Nepal, books are a luxury, as many Nepalese are either illiterate or unable to afford them.

The words used when talking to people depends on their status relative to the speaker. "Higher" words are used with people one should show respect to and "lower" words with people who should show respect to the speaker. That means children will use one grammatical form to ask their parents a question; the parents, in turn, will use another form in reply.

The same is the case at work. Bosses will use words and forms that will leave no doubt in their subordinates' minds as to who is the boss. With their own superiors, on the other hand, bosses will use words that show respect.

WRITING

The Devanagari script is very old. It is the same script used to write Hindi. Each character represents a sound, not a letter. Words are formed by joining the characters with a line across the top. The Nepalese write below the line on lined paper.

Nepal is a nation of linguists. It is not uncommon for even young children to speak two or three different languages. Most children start out speaking their own group's language at home, then learn Nepali in school. They usually pick up Hindi as they grow up. In school, they also study English.

THE DIFFERENT PERSONS IN YOU

There are many different ways to say "you" in Nepali, depending on the level of respect you should show, or want to show, the person you are talking to.

yaahaa ("yah-HAH")	Very polite.
hajur ("hah-JOOR")	Polite, often used by a woman when talking to her husband.
tapaai ("tah-PIE")	The most common form used in everyday conversation with casual friends or shopkeepers.
timi ("TEE-mee")	Used with good friends, children, or lower caste people, sometimes used by a husband with his wife. It can imply affection or a sense of superiority or both.
ta ("tah")	Used with animals, young children, people of very low status, or someone you want to fight with. It can imply great affection or a total lack of respect.

OTHER LANGUAGES

The hill groups and Bhotes speak Tibeto-Burmese languages. These languages are slightly similar to Chinese in that they are monosyllabic and tonal. To speak correctly, the right stress and tone, either rising or falling, must be used. The same syllable may have several meanings based on the stress given to the sound when speaking.

The Bhote languages, in particular, are very close to Tibetan and use the Tibetan script.

Newari, the language of the Newar, is an Indo-European language that has absorbed a great deal of influence from the Tibeto-Burmese languages. It is one of the most difficult languages in the world to learn.

People in the *terai* speak a great number of Indo-European languages. After Nepali, the two most widely spoken languages are Bhojpuri and Maithili. These languages are very different from Nepali. Although the languages have common roots, a Nepali speaker and a Maithili speaker will have a very difficult time understanding one another.

Scriptures are inscribed by a mountain pass to praise god and to protect those who travel on this precarious path.

NEPALI LITERATURE

Twentieth-century Nepalese writers mainly wrote about conditions in Nepalese society.

One of the 20th century's most famous writers was Bal Krishna Sama (1903–81). Born to a rich, aristocratic Rana family, he was appalled by the abuses committed by the Rana regime against the common Nepalese people. He changed his title to *sama*, which means "equal," as a way of bridging the gap between his privileged status and that of the rest of the Nepalese population. His novels, poetry, and essays, published in the 1920s and 1930s, draw from both Sanskrit and English literary traditions.

A contemporary of Sama, poet Laksmiprasad Devkota (1909–59) was also influenced by the literary traditions of the West, particularly poetry, tragic drama, and the short story.

NEPALI PROVERBS

What is something totally insignificant? It is "a cumin seed on an elephant's trunk." The Nepalese have all kinds of proverbs and sayings that reflect the world they live in. Some of them are easy for us to understand, while others require a little reflection:

- He can't face a live tiger, but he'll pull the whiskers off a dead one.
- He couldn't see a buffalo on himself, but he'll find a louse on someone else.
- Too many cats kill no mice.
- If you need a drink, you have to find a spring.
- Give someone a drink, but don't show them the spring.
- No one sits by a burnt-out fire.
- A knot tied with a laugh is untied with tears.
- Dress according to the land you are in.
- It takes a hundred more lies to hide the first.
- The sun can't be covered with your hand.
- The carpenter's staircase is broken.
- The elephant went through, but its tail was caught.

ARTS

IN KATHMANDU it is easy to walk past a 1,000-year-old statue without even noticing it. As daily life swirls around, the Nepalese treat masterpieces in wood, stone, metal, and brick with the casualness of an old friend. It may be hard for Westerners, used to hushed, pristine museums, to understand. But for the Nepalese, great works of art are as much a part of daily life as the morning cup of tea. To Nepalese, their art is not to be locked away and viewed from a distance on special occasions; it is an inherent part of their daily environment, to be touched, sat on, worshiped, or even used to entertain little children.

Nepal's greatest fine arts are found in the forms of sculpture and architecture. There is almost no secular art. Most Nepali art is generated for worshiping in the two great religious traditions that shape so much of life in the country—Hinduism and Buddhism.

Nepali art is mostly anonymous. We know the names of the patrons who commissioned the works, but not the names of the artists and craftsmen who executed them.

This is not the case with popular music. Songwriters are household names, and the favorite subject by far is romance. Nepalese children are brought up to sing and dance without being self-conscious. The ability to sing with wit and dance with grace often helps adult Nepalese attract and win the heart of that special someone.

In a country largely free of television and radio, the Nepalese still rely on each other's artistic talent for entertainment.

Opposite: **A dancer and his mask. The growing tourism industry has led artisans to mass-produce Nepali art.**

Below: **The *garuda* ("gah-ROO-dah") is a mythical bird from the religious drama the *Ramayana*. *Garuda* sculptures can be found in other Asian countries of Hindu influence, though the sculptures do not look exactly alike.**

A group of Newar musicians move in a procession as they play during a religious festival.

MUSIC

The Nepalese love music. Walk through any village and you are bound to hear the voice of someone singing, the lilting sound of a flute, or the catchy rhythm of a drum. Radios are becoming more common, but still, in most places in Nepal, if you want to hear music, you must play it yourself.

A wedding would not be a wedding in Nepal without a band announcing the approach of the wedding party. In the far west the band consists mostly of drummers. In the Middle Hills people play the *shanai* ("shah-NYE"), an oboe-like instrument, and big horns that curve back and over. In the cities, bands with Western instruments blast out Western and Hindi pop songs in a style that is half-polka, half-Dixieland, and all fun.

The hymns and religious songs sung at temples are accompanied by drums, large and tiny cymbals, flutes, and harmoniums. In Buddhist monasteries high in the Himalayas, monks stand on rooftops to play huge horns that are 10 to 15 feet (3 to 4.5 m) long. Their low bass rumble echoes through the high mountain valleys and can be heard for miles.

SONG

Singing is almost a national sport in Nepal. A singing competition is always one of the main attractions at festivals in the Middle Hills.

There are two teams—a boys' team and a girls' team. One side sings a short verse, asking rhetorical questions, criticizing the other team's song or dress or telling a story. As one team sings, the other must think up a wittier and more poetic reply. Onlookers offer judgments. Highest marks go to the wittiest verses. The singing may go back and forth all night without a winner. It may end with an agreement to continue the competition at the same place, same time, the following year.

One of the great traditions of Nepali music, and one that is fast disappearing, is *gaini* ("GUY-nee"). *Gaini* are wandering musicians who travel from town to town and sing for their supper. They sing about famous old stories or the latest rumors and gossip. They make a living from the donations given by the crowd of villagers who gather to listen. Long ago, *gaini* families traveled together, the children learning the songs at their father's knee.

There are nationwide competitions every year for folk songs. The wit and poetry of the verses are as important as the melody and the singer's voice.

A religious dance performed once every 12 years. The masks represent different Hindu gods and goddesses.

DRAMA

Traditional dramas retell the two great epics, the Ramayana and the Mahabharata. These dramas are performed during religious festivals and are sponsored by religious organizations.

Comedy has a long tradition in Nepal, and no drama would be complete without a comic interlude or two, sometimes even three. In recent years comic reviews have toured larger cities and have met with great success.

The biggest comedy event of the year occurs during the Gai Jatra festival. Held at the Royal Academy in Kathmandu, it is the one day of the year when you can poke fun at anything or anybody, even big and powerful public figures. There are no rules; anything can be said and no one can take offense. The results are uproarious, and cassette recordings of the evening are always bestsellers.

Nepal also has a growing modern drama movement. Modern drama deals mainly with social issues and the new problems confronting Nepal's increasingly urban, Western-influenced population—youthful alienation, evil schemers, drugs, and even topics such as government corruption and the position of women in society.

DANCE

Religious dances are very common in Nepal. The dancers wear elaborate costumes and huge masks and headdresses. Their dances depict the struggles and triumphs of the gods over demons. Religious dancers walk through the streets and dance at the temples and the old palace during the Indra Jatra ("IN-drah JAH-trah") festival.

Buddhists have a strong tradition of religious dances. Twice a year, in the Mount Everest area, the Sherpas hold a three-day epic dance re-enacting the triumph of Buddhism over the old Bon religion. People from all over the world come to see the elaborate costumes and masks and the elegant, controlled energy of the dancers.

Every ethnic group in Nepal has its own style of folk dancing. Himalayan people put their arms around each other's shoulders and form a sort of chorus line. Rai and Limbu hold hands (both men and women) and dance slowly in a circle.

In caste Hindu culture, men and women rarely dance together; women rarely dance at all. Traditionally, one or two men will dance surrounded by a close circle of people singing, clapping, and urging the swirling dancers on.

In this Gurung village, two young girls dance the story of an ancient king and queen. Because of the influence of pop culture, many young Nepalese are turning away from local traditions.

Brahmin priests sing and recite verses from a religious song they have composed and published. They will try to sell the books to the crowds that have gathered to hear them.

LITERATURE

Nepal is a nation of poets. Several poetry competitions are held each year. These competitions are often broadcast on the radio, and with the start of television broadcasting in some areas in the late 1980s, the finals are now shown on the small screen as well.

Birthdays of most famous poets are celebrated with parades and recitations of their poems. Laksmiprasad Devkota is considered one of Nepal's greatest poets. The royal family also writes poetry. Several of the late queen's poems have become popular songs.

Brahmins, members of the religious caste, sometimes privately publish a booklet of long, original poems. They recite their poems in public, singing them to a simple melody, and sell the booklets to the audience gathered around them. These poems are usually religious sermons, using a story to illustrate Hindu scriptures.

THE MAHABHARATA AND THE RAMAYANA

These Hindu epics combine the teachings of the Vedas with great stories and legends. They have been entertaining and teaching children and adults alike for thousands of years. Present-day Nepalese children can still recount the adventures of their favorite heroes.

Like the Greek *Iliad,* the stories have a basis in both myth and history, with the gods and goddesses playing an active role in the affairs of people. The Mahabharata recounts the heroic struggle of five brothers, the Pandava, against their five evil cousins. Within the Mahabharata, the Bhagavad Gita ("Song of God"), presents the essence of Hinduism.

The Ramayana centers on the adventures of the great hero Ram, his wife Sita, and his brother Laxman. Sita is kidnapped by the terrible demon Ravenna. After much searching, Ram's friend, the monkey king Hanuman, finds her on the island of Sri Lanka. Following a terrific battle, Ram finally kills the demon and rescues Sita with Hanuman's help.

Nepal figures in both epics. The great Nepalese king, Yalambar, is killed in the Mahabharata's climactic battle. In the Ramayana, Ram wins Sita's hand in marriage in a competition in Sita's home, Janakpur, in Nepal's *terai.*

The Buddhist "wheel of life" is painted in the style of Tibetan Buddhist scrolls called *thangka*.

PAINTING

There are two main painting traditions in Nepal, one with roots in the south and the other found in the north. Paintings are also mainly devoted to religious themes.

Newari paintings from as far back as the 11th century show southern influences. These paintings are miniatures used to illustrate manuscripts, and the style is derived from Indian art. By the 15th century, Brahmanic manuscripts were being beautifully decorated with miniatures done in a style similar to India's *pahari* ("pah-HAH-ree"). The painters were *Chitrakars* ("CHEE-trah-kerhs"), meaning they belonged to the painter caste in the rigid caste system in effect under the Malla kings.

Around the 14th century, Nepalese artists traveled to Tibet and across Central Asia and brought a new art form back to Nepal. Inspired by Tibetan scroll paintings called *thangka* ("TAHNG-kah"), which depict the Buddha and other Buddhist themes such as the "wheel of life," Nepalese painters began to work on scrolls. Rich in color, elaborate in design, and extremely detailed, Tibetan *thangka*-style paintings are today becoming popular in the West.

Newari paintings, *paubha* ("POW-bah") or *pati* ("PAH-tee"), also use religious themes but are not as popular with tourists.

SCULPTURE

Nepalese sculpture reached its peak during the reign of the Malla kings from the 15th to the 17th centuries. Most of the carvings were made by Newar craftsmen to decorate palaces and temples. Back then, being a sculptor was not considered a respectable profession. Therefore, the names of the master artists who created these beautiful statues are not known.

Nepal boasts stone sculpture from the sixth century, and the wooden figures on some of the temples are more than 900 years old.

Sculptors of old worked with wood, stone, and metal (usually brass). But they liked to work with metal best. They used the lost wax method, making a wax model to make a clay mold, both of which were destroyed when the statue was made. Another popular technique used a hammer and chisel to tap and pound a design into a sheet of metal, usually copper.

Both of these methods are still in use today. Visitors walking down the streets of Patan will hear the clinking sound of craftmen's hammers tapping on metal.

Nepalese craftsmen still work in the traditional manner. A large share of the pieces are made for the tourist market.

ORIGINS OF THE PAGODA

At the end of the 13th century, a master Nepalese architect, known today as Arniko, traveled north at the invitation of the Tibetans. As he and his team of 24 assistants completed several projects, Arniko's reputation spread and came to the attention of the Ming emperor of China. Arniko joined the court of the emperor, and one of his buildings still stands in Beijing. The style of pagodas (*left*) seen today all throughout East Asia owes its origins to this remarkable and little-known man.

ARCHITECTURE

Religious architecture is Nepal's main contribution to world art. Seven places in the Kathmandu Valley have been designated world heritage landmarks by the United Nations Educational, Scientific and Cultural Organization (UNESCO). No other place in the world can boast so many landmarks in such a small area.

Much of Nepal's distinctive architecture was the work of Newar artisans during the 17th and 18th centuries when craftsmen were paid from the state treasury. They built with brick, wood, and stone, so today the palace squares remain much as they were centuries ago. Most of these buildings are located in the Durbar squares of Bhaktapur, Kathmandu, and Patan.

In the 19th and 20th centuries, the Rana prime ministers filled Kathmandu with huge, European-style palaces. The largest of these palaces have been made into government offices and hotels.

In the Buddhist areas of Nepal, structures that are half-sculpture, half-architecture, called stupas, can be found. Two of the largest are located at Bodhanath and Swayambhu in the Kathmandu Valley.

Housing architecture varies from region to region. In the dry Himalayan region, roofs are flat and covered with dirt. In the Middle Hills, round, thatched roofs keep out the monsoon rains. In the *terai,* houses are raised on stilts to protect them from floods caused by the monsoon, to catch cool breezes during the hot summer months, and to keep wild animals out.

Stupas are Buddhist representations of the universe. The mound represents earth, water, air, and fire. The eyes are those of the Buddha. The third eye is the eye of true knowledge. The nose is the number 1 and represents unity. The 13 rings of the spire are the 13 degrees of knowledge. The ladder to Nirvana is represented by an umbrella-like structure at the top.

LEISURE

LIFE IN NEPAL MOVES at a slower pace than it does in the United States or Europe. There are no shopping malls, and most stores are a single small room, stocked with the basic necessities.

Television reaches only a small portion of the population in Kathmandu and the *terai* area and broadcasts for only a few hours a day. There is one radio station, which also broadcasts for only part of the day. Parks and sports fields are found in just a few cities. There are dozens of newspapers, but distribution is slow and limited. Other reading material is scarce.

What do people do when they are not working? Mostly people like to relax and hang out, talking to friends, listening to other people talking to their friends, sipping a cup of milk tea in the village tea shop, and watching people walk by.

Some lie down in a cool, shady spot and take a nap; others just sit under a tree and wait for a friend to come by so that they can exchange the latest village gossip.

Above: **Nepali chess, or** *bhaagh-chaal* **("bug-chal"), uses pieces shaped like tigers and goats. Often stones are used as a substitute for the pieces.**

Opposite: **A flute seller in Kathmandu.**

Left: **Soccer is played in Nepal's urban areas. It is not as popular in the hills because of the lack of flat land in that region.**

MOVIES

Going to the movies is a favorite pastime. Nepalese will sometimes pay three to four times the price for tickets to a popular movie on the black market.

Nepalese love to go to the movies. Every large town with access to electricity has a theater of some kind. Movies are a great bargain—the best seats cost only about USD 30 cents. Most of the movies are imported from India and are in Hindi. Since Hindi is very similar to Nepali, most Nepalese have no problem understanding the dialogue.

Hindi movies can be enjoyed even without understanding the language. The plots are simple and direct, the bad guys are really bad, the heroines are beautiful, and the heroes are almost supermen.

Movies last about three hours and have a little bit of everything in them—tragedy, comedy, rock'em-sock'em fights, and spectacular musical numbers—and often switch from one to the other in the space of a few seconds. The seats may be backless benches, the theater may be as hot as an oven, and the projector bulb may blow every 10 minutes, but movies are still great entertainment.

Video is bringing movies to even the most remote villages. Porters will carry a television, a videocassette recorder, and a small generator for days through the hills, turning the school hall of each village into a temporary theater. The entire village will turn out to watch. Many villagers have never been to the movies. At first they may not even understand the images on the screen, but like anywhere else, they quickly become movie fans.

MODERN SPORTS

Volleyball is the most popular sport in the hills because it does not require a large playing field. In the *terai* and larger valleys, soccer is also popular. There are several national club tournaments, and teams from all over Asia are invited to take part. Cricket is played in some large towns.

In the 1988 Seoul Olympics, a Nepalese boxer won Nepal's first and only Olympic medal ever, a bronze. The martial arts, particularly tae-kwon-do, are becoming very popular, and Nepalese players are now strong contestants in all-Asian competitions.

TRADITIONAL PASTIMES AND SPORTS

With no spare money to spend on elaborate equipment, most Nepali games only require what can be recycled from home or the ground.

One of the most popular children's game is *dhandi-biu* ("DHAHN-dee byoo"). A bat-like stick is used to flick the end of a small seed lying on the ground, flipping it into the air. The player tries to tap the seed twice while it is still in the air, and then hit it as far as possible. The farthest hit wins.

Kite flying is also popular. Nepali kites have no tails and control is difficult. Once up in the air, kites fight each other. The goal is to use your kite's string to snap the string of your opponent's kite.

Nepal's most famous game, *baagh-chaal,* meaning "tigers and goats," is played on a board. The object of the game is for the tigers to eat up all the goats by jumping over them onto an open space or for the goats to trap all the tigers by preventing the tigers from moving.

Nepal's traditional national sport is *kabaddi* ("KAH-bahd-dee"), which originated in India. Two teams of boys face each other across a line on the ground. A player from team A rushes across the line and attempts to tag one of the players on team B, while saying "*kabaddi.*" The players on team B try to avoid the tag, but if one of them is tagged, they rush to stop their opponent from recrossing the line. If they can hold him until he runs out of breath and stops yelling "*kabaddi,*" they win; he wins if he recrosses the line. There is a similar game for all-girl teams. National tournaments for both sexes are held every year.

THE MELA

Local festivals called *mela* ("MAY-lah") are a source of leisure for all Nepalese. *Mela* are religious celebrations, but the atmosphere is more like a carnival. The date of the *mela* is based on the phases of the moon, usually a full moon or new moon, or halfway between. No special activities take place at the *mela*. It is just a time for people to get together and have fun.

Often, people will walk for days to go to a good *mela*. At the *mela*, people get a chance to see friends from other villages, to eat foods they cannot eat everyday, and to buy clothes or jewelry. Men gamble; women gossip and shop. Young people sing, dance, and court, and small children do not worry about bedtime. Sometimes a porter carries in a videocassette recorder and generator, and two or three movies will be shown repeatedly for as long as fuel for the generator lasts.

Mela can last from one to several days. Each community will hold its own *mela*, providing entertainment at intervals throughout the year. *Mela* are usually held near rivers or streams.

FESTIVALS

NEPAL HAS DOZENS OF FESTIVALS. If you include local festivals, it is safe to say that every day of the year there is a festival taking place somewhere in Nepal. Although there are some secular holidays, all the major holidays and festivals are based on religious celebrations.

Many festivals are dedicated to the worship of a god or goddess. Shiva Raatri ("SHEE-vah RAH-tree"), for example, is dedicated to the Hindu god Shiva. Some festivals have a more human face. Bhai Tika ("bhye TEE-kah") is a festival for family members, and Tij ("teej") is for women only.

Each religious group in Nepal celebrates its own religious holidays; few festivals are observed nationwide. Dasain, the biggest Hindu holiday, is not celebrated by Buddhists. Losar ("LOH-sahr"), New Year's Day and the biggest holiday for the Himalayan people, is not celebrated by the rest of the population. Indra Jatra is observed only in the Kathmandu Valley.

In the Himalayan area, most Buddhist monasteries hold annual dance festivals in the monastery's courtyard. Dancers in elaborate costumes and masks enact fables and legends, providing both entertainment and moral education.

Most towns hold one big festival, or *mela*, every year. Overnight, small stalls selling food and trinkets spring up in an open field. People walk all day, eat, sing, dance, and gamble all night, then walk back home. The largest *mela* is the Tribeni Mela held under the full moon in February. Over 100,000 people gather for this one-day fair.

Opposite: **A chariot is pulled along the streets in Bhaktapur during the Biskhet festival to celebrate the Nepali New Year.**

Below: **A joker in the Gai Jatra Festival. During this event, people are given the opportunity to poke fun at just about anything.**

CALENDAR OF ANNUAL FESTIVALS

Festival dates are determined using Nepal's lunar calendar.
Thus the dates change every year on the Western calendar.

December–January   Seto Machhendranath

The Holy Month of Magh

February–March   Shiva Raatri (Shiva's Night)

Tribhuvan Jayanti

March–May   Baleju Jatra

Ghora Jatra

Biskhet Jatra

Mother's Day

Raato Machhendranath

Buddha Jayanti (Buddha's Birthday)

May–August   Mani Rimdu (*right*)

Naga Panchami (Day of the Snakes)

Janai Pumima

August–September   Gai Jatra

Krishna Jayanti (Krishna's Birthday)

Father's Day

Tij

September–October   Indra Jatra

Dasain

Tihar (Festival of Lights)

November–December Sita Bibha Panchami

Bala Chaturdasi

TIHAR—FESTIVAL OF LIGHTS

Tihar celebrations are somewhat like Christmas celebrations. There are gifts, decorated houses lit at night, special foods, and even a special nocturnal visitor—Laxmi, goddess of wealth and good fortune.

Five creatures are worshiped during Tihar. On the first day, food is left out for crows. On the second day, dogs are given flower necklaces and *tika* and fed at a banquet. Cows, symbols of Laxmi, are bathed and garlanded on the third day, and bullocks on the fourth. On the fifth day, the last creatures, people, receive blessings to remain healthy.

At midnight of the third day, Laxmi visits deserving homes. Houses are cleaned and decorated with tinsel and lights. Families prepare to receive Laxmi by painting a path leading from the door to where the home's valuables are placed and adorning it with oil lamps. They place a burning lamp, some flowers, and food for Laxmi beside the valuables table. Children set off fireworks.

Women of the neighborhood go singing from house to house and are rewarded with presents. On the following night, it is the men's turn to go out singing.

During Tihar, Nepal's cities and towns are ablaze with lights to guide the goddess of wealth to people's homes.

On the fourth day, homes are lit again. The Newar celebrate their New Year's Day on this day. On the fifth day, men and boys receive the *Bhai Tika*, or "brother's blessing," from their sisters. This blessing is so important that even if a sister has moved far away to another village, men will travel to the sister's home to receive the blessing. If a boy does not have a sister, a relative will act the part. In return for the blessing, the sister receives gifts.

TIJ—FESTIVAL FOR WOMEN

During Tij, women dress up in bright red saris after having their ritual bath in the river.

Although it means fasting for at least a day, women in Nepal look forward to the three days of Tij. It is their only break from household duties. On the first day the women of the household eat a fine feast, sparing no expense as they must fast on the second day.

The fast reenacts Parbati's fast, when she prayed that the god Shiva would marry her. Shiva did marry her, and in return, Parbati promised that any woman who fasted would be blessed with a good marriage and many children.

All day, groups of women gather by rivers and streams. After bathing, they dress in their best clothes, usually a bright red sari, and worship Shiva. Then they gather with friends and neighbors to sing and dance into the night.

On the morning of the third day, each woman makes an offering of food to her husband and breaks her fast. A ritual bath ends the festival.

SHIVA RAATRI—SHIVA'S NIGHT

Each February, tens of thousands of Nepalese come to the Kathmandu Valley to bathe in the Bagmati River at the point where it flows by Pashupati Temple. Devotees come from India and all over Nepal on the 14th day of the waning moon.

Long ago, on this date, Shiva is supposed to have spent a whole night here in meditation. He is said to love the spot so much that he returns every year on the same night to meditate. People who spend the night in meditation and then bathe at dawn are supposed to gain the god's favor.

On Shiva's night, the woods near the temple become a huge campground, lit with the fires of thousands of pilgrims, chanting and trying to keep warm throughout the night. In February the temperature may be 32°F (0°C) and the water is freezing cold. Bathing is no easy thing to do.

At the first light of dawn, people start bathing in the icy river. They stand in line for hours to pour a little of the river's water over a stone *lingam* ("LING-gum"), a fertility symbol representing Shiva.

People throng to bathe along the river by Pashupati Temple in celebration of Shiva Raatri.

THE KUMARI

The Kumari ("koo-MAH-ree") is believed to be the goddess Kanya Kumari in human form. The Kumari is chosen at the age of about 4 from the Sakya clan of gold- and silversmiths.

Her body must have 32 special signs and cannot have any flaws or scars. She must identify items known only to the Kumari. Lastly, she must walk fearlessly through a dark room filled with men in demon masks and bloody buffalo heads. If she fulfills all of these requirements and can endure the last test, she is the Kumari, the Living Goddess.

The Kumari moves into a palace, where she lives like a queen. She is forbidden to leave except on a few special occasions. Even then, she is carried (*below*) because her feet must never touch the ground.

She remains the Kumari until she loses blood, either from a cut or on reaching puberty. Then she returns to her own family, an ordinary person again. Many ex-Kumaris find this transition from divinity back to being a mortal very difficult to make. For some, being the Kumari becomes a stigma, not a blessing.

INDRA JATRA

The Indra Jatra, which lasts eight days, is the main festival of the Kathmandu Valley. Long ago, Indra, the god of rain, came to the valley to steal some beautiful flowers. He was caught by the people and tied in heavy ropes like a common man. It was not until Indra's mother came to seek him and convinced the people of Indra's true identity that they released him. In return, she gave the people two gifts. She would take to heaven all who died that year and she would give the valley wet, foggy winter mornings to help moisten the crops.

During the festival, beautifully costumed and masked dancers wander through Kathmandu, reenacting the search for Indra.

For three nights during the festival, the Kumari, the Living Goddess, is carried through the streets in her chariot. On the second night, as thousands wait, the Kumari gives a *tika* to the king. This rite symbolizes the goddess' blessing on the king, thus ensuring continued prosperity for the kingdom.

Indra Jatra is also used to worship another god, the terrible Bhairav ("BHYE-rahv") the Destroyer. Every neighborhood puts a mask of this terrifying deity on display. The climax of this celebration begins at night, when rice beer flows out from a large mask of Bhairav and crowds of young men wrestle to take a drink.

From the huge mouth of a Bhairav mask flows rice beer. A small fish is to be found somewhere in the flow. To drink the fish is to have guaranteed prosperity for the following year.

Items used for worship during Dasain. The curved knife at the top is called a *khukuri*.

DASAIN

Dasain is the most important festival to Nepalese Hindus. All offices and stores are closed for most of this 11-day celebration. Nepalese living away from their home village will go to great lengths to return home. All workers receive a bonus. Special foods are made and new clothes bought.

Dasain celebrates the victory of good over evil, represented by the victory of the goddess Durga ("DUR-gah") over the demon Mahisasura ("mah-hee-sah-SOO-rah"), who terrorized the earth in the form of a huge water buffalo. Durga, the wife of Shiva, is often illustrated riding a tiger or a lion, her arms filled with the weapons she used to defeat Mahisasura, who lies prostrate at her feet.

On the first day of Dasain, each household plants barley seeds. On the ninth day, each household sacrifices an animal—a fowl, goat, or water buffalo—by slitting its throat or beheading it with a large *khukuri*. The blood from the animal is dripped over vehicles to ensure Durga's protection for the coming year. The sacrifices are followed by a big feast.

The actual victory of Durga over the demon is celebrated on the 10th celebration day. Everyone puts on new clothes and visits relatives and friends to exchange greetings and *tika*. On the 11th day, the barley, which has grown into bright green sprouts, is distributed to every member of the family by the head of the household. The barley is placed on the head as a sign of blessing.

Goddess Durga rides her tiger in a triumphant attitude after defeating evil. Nepalese celebrate her victory during Dasain, Nepal's biggest festival.

Once a year, the Raato Machendranath ("RAH-toe mah-CHEHN-dreh-naht") is paraded through the city of Patan. Believers rush forward to touch it and pray for good fortune.

RAATO MACHENDRANATH

Every year, starting in late April, the city of Patan celebrates its biggest festival in honor of the god Raato ("red") Machendra. The image of the god, painted red and decorated with jewels and flower garlands, is taken from

his temple and placed in a wagon topped by a 40-foot (12-m) pointed structure covered with pine. The wagon is pulled slowly by over a hundred men through the narrow streets of Patan, stopping for the night in every neighborhood to give people the chance to worship. It can take a month or more for the wagon to travel through the city. Often, the wagon collides with houses and the wheels get stuck in gutters. Each neighborhood takes turns to feed and care for the men pulling the wagon.

The climax comes in an open field around late May. Thousands of people come to see and cheer the king of Nepal as he displays a sacred vest believed to have been given to the Raato Machendranath by the Serpent King. The Nepalese, largely a farming people, believe that the Raato Machendranath controls the monsoon rains, and that the vest guarantees plenty of rain for the coming rice-planting season in June.

BUDDHIST HOLIDAYS

LOSAR The most important festival in the Himalayan area is Losar, or New Year's Day. It is a time for dressing up in new clothes, visiting family and friends, and eating and drinking to one's heart's content.

At Bodhanath near Kathmandu, big crowds string prayer flags from the *stupa*. A photo of the Dalai Lama, the spiritual leader of Tibetan Buddhists, is paraded through the crowd.

At the climax, an exact moment determined by astrologers, everyone hurls handfuls of *tsampa* ("SAHM-pah") flour, made from roasted barley, into the air, then at each other. Groups of people form long lines, with arms over each other's shoulders, and dance in a slow shuffle.

BUDDHA JAYANTI ("Buddha JYAIN-tee") On the full moon in April or early May, the birth of the Buddha is celebrated by Nepal's Buddhist community. People make pilgrimages to a monastery, where lamas hold special services. It is also a time for feasts and visiting friends and relatives. In Kathmandu, Swayambhu Temple is the center of the celebrations, with thousands of people climbing the 300 steep stairs that lead to the top to worship at the many shrines around the *stupa*.

Color badges used during the festival of Raksha Bandhan. Traditionally, a girl ties the badge around her brother's wrist as a sign of affection.

FESTIVALS OF THE FAMILY AND HOME

DASAIN and **BHAI TIKA** are festivals that combine the worship of a god and goddess with a celebration that strengthens family ties. The main purpose of several other festivals is to strengthen the ties between family and home; these festivals are celebrated mostly within the family.

MOTHER'S DAY In Nepal, Mother's Day is called *Aamaa-ko mukh herne din*, literally "see mother's face day." All children, including those that have married and moved away (usually daughters), return home to visit their mother. They present sweets, fruit, and other gifts to their mother and, as a sign of respect, bend down so that their forehead touches her feet. The mother blesses them by placing her hand on their forehead.

FATHER'S DAY Called *Buaa-ko mukh herne din*, Father's Day is celebrated in much the same way as Mother's Day.

A picture of Krishna with the Serpent King behind him.

RAKSHA BANDHAN ("RAHK-shyah BAHN-dhahn") Girls tie decorated silk threads around their brothers' right wrist and give the *tika* as signs of sisterly affection and devotion. In return, their brothers give them gifts and promise to look after them all their life.

NAGA PANCHAMI ("NAH-gah PAHN-chyah-mee") Houses in Nepal are usually built from clay bricks or mud and rocks. During heavy monsoon rains, many of the houses collapse. Nepalese believe angry snake gods living in the ground beneath the house cause it to collapse. To keep the snake gods happy, on Naga Panchami, every family hangs a picture of the Serpent King and his retainers above the main door of the house. A bright red *tika* is placed on the Serpent King's forehead. They pray to the snakes and place offerings of milk, honey, curd, and rice outside the house.

FOOD

WHEN TWO NEPALESE meet on the road, the first question they will ask is *"Bhaat khanu bhaeyo?"* ("bhaht khahn-noo bhye-yoh"), meaning "have you eaten rice?" This shows the importance Nepalese place on eating rice. Often, Nepalese use the word *khanaa* ("khahn-nah"), meaning "food," when they are talking about *bhaat*, or rice. Rice is the staple food, but in most of the country, rice is a luxury and a sign of wealth and status.

Rice can only grow at altitudes of up to about 6,000 feet (1,829 m), and it needs lots of water. Most of Nepal does not meet these conditions. In many places rice is transported to small villages carried on someone's back, raising its price so much that many people can only eat rice on special occasions.

Most Nepalese depend on other grains—wheat, corn, and millet at low and middle altitudes and barley and buckwheat at high altitudes. The grain is ground into a flour by hand or at a mill, then boiled into a thick paste or made into *roti* ("ROH-tee"), a bread.

Nutritious and tasty, the classic Nepalese meal is *dal bhaat tarkaari* ("dahl bhaht tahr-KAH-ree")—lentil soup, rice, and curried vegetables. Lentils provide protein, rice is the carbohydrate, and vegetables provide vitamins and minerals. Neither meat nor eggs are part of the daily meal. Milk and curd are more common, but not served every day in most homes. *Achaar* ("ah-CHAHR"), pickled vegetables, is a popular side dish.

Opposite: **A Nepali feast fit for a king. Most Nepalese eat this kind of meal only during feasts or other very special occasions.**

Below: **A group of Gurung women harvesting millet. Later, the millet grains will be either ground to make flour or fermented to produce liquor.**

Fiery red chilies are dried in the sun. They will be blended with other spices to flavor curries.

FOOD CUSTOMS

Food is only eaten with the right hand—the "clean" hand. Nepalese wash their hands before and after they eat.

During a meal, Nepalese pour some lentil soup over a portion of rice. They mix the soup and rice using their right hand, form it into a bite-sized portion, and pop it into their mouth. Then they eat some of the vegetables, pickles, or other side dishes. To a Nepalese, *dal bhaat tarkaari* eaten with the hand tastes better than when eaten with a spoon.

All the food on a plate becomes *jutho* ("JYOO-toh"), or "contaminated," when even the tiniest piece of food has been eaten. To offer leftovers to another person is a huge insult. Any food not eaten is given to the animals. This taboo is not as strong with people living in the Himalayas.

Meals are eaten twice a day, in the mid-morning and in the evening before bedtime, with a simple snack in between. Hindus are forbidden by their religion from eating beef. Brahmins have many dietary restrictions. They should not eat chicken, duck, buffalo, onions, leeks, mushrooms, and tomatoes. All foods are classified as "hot" or "cold" based on their effect on the body. Mango is hot; yogurt is cold.

Water is usually drunk from a communal pitcher. If a person's mouth touches the pitcher, the pitcher becomes *jutho* and must be thrown away.

People drink by pouring water into their open mouth and swallowing at the same time.

Just before rice is placed on a plate, the plate is rinsed with water. A dry plate is considered unclean.

Before serving rice, Nepalese throw a few grains of rice into the fire as an offering to the gods.

Nepalese do not eat dessert. After a meal, they chew a piece of betel nut, clove, or cardamom.

EVERYDAY FOODS

Nepal's main vegetable is potato, which is found almost everywhere. Spinach and squash are also common. Vegetables like onions and carrots are rare, except in major towns.

There are no refrigerators and no canned food in Nepal. In rural areas, vegetables are cooked as soon as they are picked. In towns, people shop every day, buying the necessary ingredients for the day's meal.

Meat is a rare treat, usually served on festive occasions. Goat is the most common type of meat. Before a goat is killed, families in the village decide how the meat will be divided.

Milk is an important source of protein. It is always boiled and served hot. Yogurt is also very popular.

Curry spices are ground together fresh on a stone for each meal. Nepalese use any of the dozens of spices sold in the market—turmeric, cumin, coriander, cardamom, pepper, fennel, fennugreek, ginger, mustard seeds, even cloves, cinnamon, and nutmeg—or homegrown spices.

This simple fruit and vegetable stand along the sidewalk displays plenty of bananas, chilies, and cherry tomatoes.

KHEER

This dish of rice cooked in milk with spices is delicious and almost a whole meal in itself. Thus it is unfair to call it simply "rice pudding." At some Newar feasts it is served instead of plain, cooked rice and eaten with meat and vegetables.

1 cup long-grain rice
$^1/_2$ cup melted butter
4 cups milk
5–10 large whole cloves
2 or 3 teaspoons cardamom seeds

1 or 2 large sticks of cinnamon, broken into pieces
1 cup light brown sugar
$^1/_2$ cup raisins
$^1/_2$ cup cashew nuts
$^1/_2$ cup shredded dried coconut

Wash and drain rice. Mix rice with melted butter. In a large, heavy saucepan bring milk to a rapid boil. Add rice. After milk boils again, turn heat down very low. Cook rice for about 10 minutes. Add spices and cook until rice is tender (about 10 more minutes). Add sugar, raisins, cashew nuts, and shredded dried coconut. Remove from heat and let rice sit tightly-covered for about 20 minutes before serving.

FOOD IN THE HIMALAYAN REGION

The food of the Himalayan area is based on several staples. One of them is butter tea. After brewing Himalayan tea, Nepalese pour it into what looks like an old-fashioned butter churn. They add butter and salt and churn the tea thoroughly. They then pour the salty, buttery tea into a jug and place it by the fire. To a foreigner, the taste may seem strange at first, but it usually gets better with every cup and can become a pleasant addiction. Healthy and hearty, Himalayan tea is drunk throughout the day and is the first thing offered to any visitor.

Tsampa, roasted barley ground into flour, is another staple food. People place the flour in a cup and mix it with butter tea into a thick paste. *Tsampa* can be made into a thick stew by adding potatoes and meat and is also made into thick *roti* and fried in butter.

The other staple is potatoes, boiled or baked in burning coals. A big plate of potatoes is a meal in itself. People eat potatoes by dipping them

With no refrigeration, dried goods are a staple food in the Nepalese diet. This store sells many kinds of dried beans, lentils, and vegetables.

in a plate of salt ground together with hot chilies.

Meat is sometimes eaten, as the dry, cold climate preserves it for months. Buddhists are allowed to eat meat, but are forbidden from killing any animals. Himalayan people often hire people from the Middle Hills to come and slaughter the animals for them.

A young man pours *chhang*, or rice beer, into a bucket.

THE NATIONAL DRINK

Tea is Nepal's national drink. In Nepal, the choices of what to add to tea go far beyond sugar, milk, or lemon. Nepalese add whatever spices they have handy. Ginger, cloves, cinnamon, cinnamon leaves, and cardamom are common additions to the teapot. Nepalese like their tea sweet, spicy, and milky. If there is no sugar, a pinch of salt is added to each cup.

On cold winter mornings, Nepalese brew raw ginger or ground black pepper in their milk tea. It is hard to imagine a more suitable drink on a cold winter morning than Nepalese-style hot, milky tea, spiced with pepper or ginger.

LIQUOR

It is illegal to make liquor in Nepal, but it is rare to find a house in Nepal, except for high-caste Hindus, that does not. There are two main types of homemade liquor—*raksi* ("RAHK-see") and *chhang* ("chahng").

Chhang is a fermented beer-like drink with a milky texture. Almost always made from rice, but sometimes also from barley, maize, rye, or millet, *chhang* is almost a meal in itself. The Sherpas like to drink it in the afternoons and evenings.

In the Middle Hills and the Himalayan area, tea and sugar may not be easily available, so the morning may start instead with a glass of warmed *raksi*. More common in the average household than *chhang*, *raksi* is a distilled drink made from any type of grain, but usually from millet. Some brews use potatoes. Water is added again after it has been distilled. It is usually drunk warm, and some butter and a few grains of roasted rice are sometimes added to give it more flavor.

Drinking is a social institution in Nepal. Nepalese usually drink liquor accompanied by a small plate of snacks—meat, if possible. Eating meals and drinking alcohol are done separately. The meal is not eaten until drinking is finished, which means the meal may be delayed until 10 or 11 at night. After eating, the evening is finished and everyone goes home or heads for bed.

A favorite drink in the east is *thoumba* ("TOOM-bah"). Fermented millet is placed in a pitcher, hot water is added, and the concoction is sipped through a bamboo straw. Water can be added two or three times, and one pitcher may last through hours of conversation.

One traditional way to determine if the liquor is strong enough is to dip one finger into the brew and then hold a lighted match to the finger. If the liquor bursts into flame, it is considered to be of sufficient strength.

DAL (LENTIL SOUP)

This recipe makes 6–8 servings.

1 cup masoor lentils*
3–4 cups water
1/2 teaspoon turmeric
1/4 teaspoon salt
1 stick cinnamon
2 cloves garlic
1 small tomato

1 small onion
2 tablespoons oil
1/2 teaspoon ground cumin
1/2 teaspoon ground coriander
Salt to taste
Yogurt (optional)

*Masoor lentils are salmon pink in color when dry, but turn yellow as they cook. If masoor lentils are not available, they may be replaced with plain lentils.

Wash lentils several times, removing any skins that come off. After draining the water away a final time, put lentils in a heavy pot with 3 cups of the water and bring to a boil. Add turmeric, 1/4 teaspoon salt, and cinnamon. Partially cover, turn down heat to a simmer, and cook for one more hour. Stir occasionally and add more water if needed. As the lentils cook, mince the garlic and chop the tomato and onion. Heat the oil in a frying pan and add garlic and onion. Cook onion until transparent and add cumin and coriander. After a few minutes, add salt to taste. Then add tomato. Stir and cook. Try and time it so that this mixture is cooked as the lentils become soupy. Add the tomato mixture to the lentil soup and stir. Add more water and salt to taste. Serve over 4 cups cooked long-grain rice. A bit of yogurt is sometimes added at the end as a special flavoring.

CHIYA (NEPALI MILK TEA)

This recipe makes 6 cups of tea.

3 cups milk
4 cloves
4 cardamom pods
4 teaspoons sugar
2 cinnamon sticks
3 cups water
4 teaspoons black tea leaves

Pour milk into a saucepan. Add cloves, cardamom pods, sugar, and cinnamon sticks. Heat milk until it comes to a boil. Let the milk simmer for a while, being careful not to burn it. In a kettle, bring water to a boil. Remove from heat and add tea leaves. Let sit for about three minutes. Carefully strain the hot milk into the tea. Gently heat for a few minutes. Do not boil, as this will make the tea bitter. Strain into tea cups and enjoy. Add more sugar if necessary. If sugar is unavailable, Nepalese sometimes add salt, pepper, or ginger to their *chiya*.

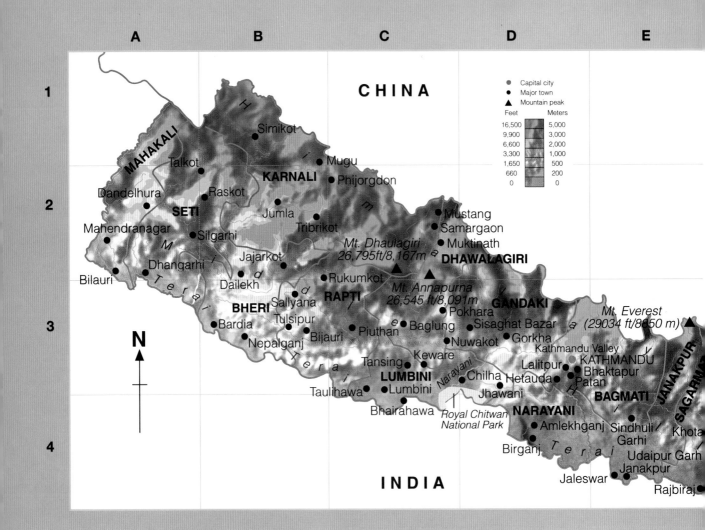

MAP OF NEPAL

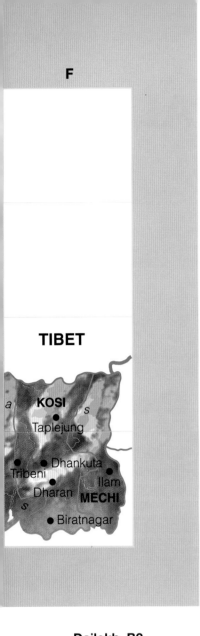

F

TIBET

a
KOSI
s
Taplejung
Dhankuta
Tribeni
Ilam
Dharan **MECHI**
s
Biratnagar

Everest, Mt., E3

Gandaki, C3, D2, D3
Gorkha, D3

Himalayan mountain
 range, B2, C2, D2,
 D3, E3, F3

Illam, F4
India, A1–A4, B3, B4,
 C4, D4, E4, F3, F4

Jajarkot, B2
Jaleswar, E4
Janakpur (city), E4
Janakpur (zone), D3,
 D4, E3, E4
Jhawani, D3
Jumla, B2

Kathmandu, D3
Kathmandu Valley,
 D3, D4
Keware, C3
Khotang, E4
Kosi, F3, F4

Lalitapur, D3
Lumbini (city), C3
Lumbini (zone), C3,
 C4, D3, D4

Mahakali, A1–A3
Mahendranagar, A2

Mechi, F3, F4
Middle Hills, A2, B2,
 B3, C3, D3, E3,
 E4, F4
Mugu, B1
Muktinath, C2
Mustang, C2

Narayani, D3, D4
Narayani River, C3,
 C4, D4
Nepalganj, B3
Nuwakot, C3

Patan, D3
Phijorgdon, C2
Piuthan, C3
Pokhara, C3

Rajbiraj, E4
Rapti, B2, B3, C2, C3
Raskot, B2
Royal Chitwan
 National Park, C3,
 C4, D3, D4

Dailekh, B2
Dandelhura, A2
Dhangarhi, A2
Dhankuta, F4
Dharan, F4
Dhaulagiri, Mt., C2
Dhawalagiri, C2, C3,
 D2

Rukumkot, B2

Sagarmatha, E3, E4,
 F3, F4
Sallyana, B3
Samargaon, C2
Seti, A1–A3, B1, B2
Silgarhi, A2
Simikot, B1
Sindhuli Garhi, E4
Sisaghat Bazar, D3

Talkot, B2
Tansing, C3
Taplejung, F3
Taulbawa, C3
Terai region, A2, A3,
 B3, C3, C4, D4,
 E4, F4
Tibet, F3
Tribeni, F4
Tribrikot, B2
Tulsipur, B3

Udaipur Garhi, E4

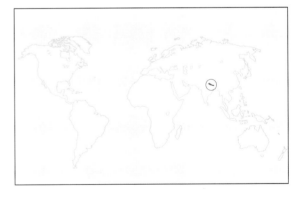

ECONOMIC NEPAL

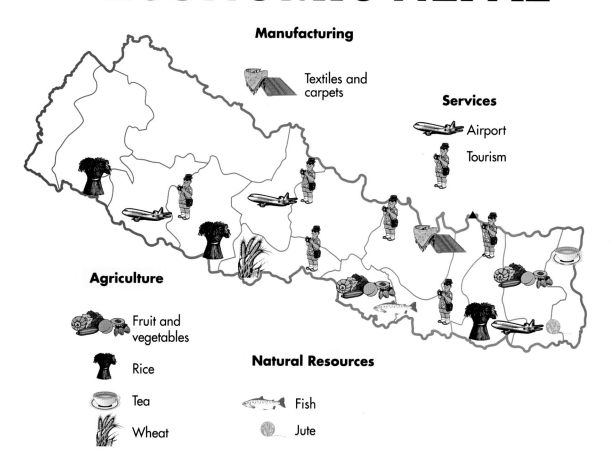

Manufacturing

Textiles and carpets

Services

Airport

Tourism

Agriculture

Fruit and vegetables

Rice

Tea

Wheat

Natural Resources

Fish

Jute

ABOUT THE ECONOMY

OVERVIEW

Nepal is one of the least developed countries in the world. Agriculture accounts for about 40 percent of the GDP. Over 80 percent of the people are farmers, but they produce barely enough to survive. Over 40 percent of Nepalese live below the poverty line. The textile and carpet industries and tourism are important activities, but the money made is used to pay for goods needed to support these industries.

POPULATION
25.3 million (July 2001)

WORKFORCE
14 million (2001)

UNEMPLOYMENT
Exact figures are not available, unemployment is a severe problem in Nepal.

GDP
$5.5 billion (2001)

EXTERNAL DEBT
$2.8 billion

LAND AREA
56,139 square miles (147,180 square km)
Nepal has no sea access.

LAND USE
Arable: 17 percent*
Pasture: 15 percent
Woodlands: 42 percent
Other: 26 percent
*About 40 percent of arable land is irrigated.

AGRICULTURAL PRODUCTS
Corn, potatoes, pulses, rice, sugarcane, wheat

NATURAL RESOURCES
Scenic beauty, timber, water (used for hydroelectric power), and small amounts of cobalt, copper, iron ore, lignite, and quartz

TOTAL EXPORTS
USD 697 million (2001)

MAJOR EXPORTS
Carpets, grains, jute and leather goods, and textiles (mainly pashmina shawls)

MAJOR EXPORT PARTNERS
India, United States, Germany

TOTAL IMPORTS
USD 1.3 billion (2001)

MAJOR IMPORTS
Fertilizer, food products, gold, machinery, and petroleum products

MAJOR IMPORT PARTNERS
India, China, Singapore

TRANSPORTATION
Highways: 2,558 miles (4,115 km) paved roads
Railways: One 37-mile (60-km) rail line
Airports: 45 airports, nine with paved runways

CURRENCY
1 Nepali rupee (NPR) = 100 paisa
Notes: 1, 2, 5, 10, 20, 50, 100, 500, 1,000
Coins: 1, 5, 10, 25, 50 paisa, 1 rupee
76 NPR = 1 USD

CULTURAL NEPAL

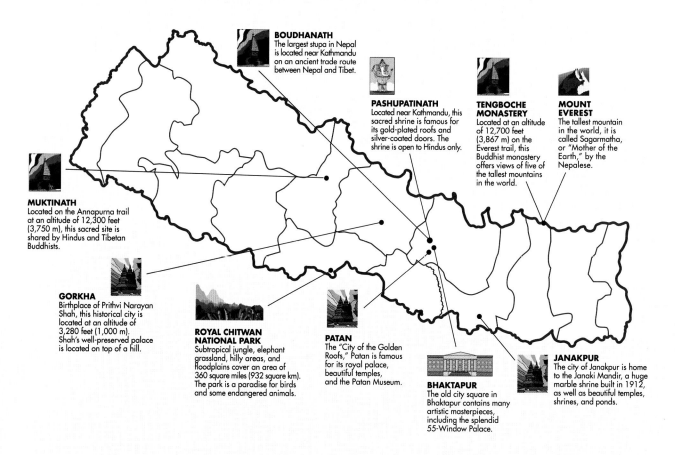

BOUDHANATH
The largest stupa in Nepal is located near Kathmandu on an ancient trade route between Nepal and Tibet.

PASHUPATINATH
Located near Kathmandu, this sacred shrine is famous for its gold-plated roofs and silver-coated doors. The shrine is open to Hindus only.

TENGBOCHE MONASTERY
Located at an altitude of 12,700 feet (3,867 m) on the Everest trail, this Buddhist monastery offers views of five of the tallest mountains in the world.

MOUNT EVEREST
The tallest mountain in the world, it is called Sagarmatha, or "Mother of the Earth," by the Nepalese.

MUKTINATH
Located on the Annapurna trail at an altitude of 12,300 feet (3,750 m), this sacred site is shared by Hindus and Tibetan Buddhists.

GORKHA
Birthplace of Prithvi Narayan Shah, this historical city is located at an altitude of 3,280 feet (1,000 m). Shah's well-preserved palace is located on top of a hill.

ROYAL CHITWAN NATIONAL PARK
Subtropical jungle, elephant grassland, hilly areas, and floodplains cover an area of 360 square miles (932 square km). The park is a paradise for birds and some endangered animals.

PATAN
The "City of the Golden Roofs," Patan is famous for its royal palace, beautiful temples, and the Patan Museum.

BHAKTAPUR
The old city square in Bhaktapur contains many artistic masterpieces, including the splendid 55-Window Palace.

JANAKPUR
The city of Janakpur is home to the Janaki Mandir, a huge marble shrine built in 1912, as well as beautiful temples, shrines, and ponds.

ABOUT THE CULTURE

OFFICIAL NAME
Kingdom of Nepal

CAPITAL
Kathmandu

LANGUAGE
Nepali, the official language, is spoken by 90 percent of the population usually as a second language. Twelve other major languages and about 30 major dialects are also spoken.

ETHNIC GROUPS

Hindus: Brahmins (priests), Chhetris (warriors), Vaisyas (merchants and farmers), and Sudras (artisans)

Newar: Kathmandu's indigenous people

Hill groups: Gurung, Limbu, Magar, Sherpa, Tamang, and Rai

LIFE EXPECTANCY

Male: 58 years
Female: 57 years

LITERACY

Male: 52 percent
Female: 18 percent

EDUCATION

Nepal has no system of compulsory education, but 64 percent of the population attends primary school, while 30 percent attends secondary school. Few Nepalese can afford to attend universities.

RELIGION

Hindu: 86.2 percent
Buddhist: 7.8 percent
Muslim: 3.8 percent
Other: 2.2 percent

LEADERS IN POLITICS

King Prithvi Narayan Shah—founder of the modern Nepali state

B.P. Koirala—tireless fighter for democracy

King Birendra—led the 1990 transition to parliamentary and constitutional democracy

LEADERS IN LITERATURE

Bal Krishna Sama—novelist, essayist, poet

Laksmiprasad Devkota—poet, short story writer

Visvesvaraprasad Koirala—short story writer

Bhavani Bhiksu—short story writer

MAJOR HOLIDAYS

July 7—King Gyanendra's birthday

August/September—*Tij* (three days of feasting, bathing, and dancing exclusively for Hindu women)

September/October—*Dasain* (11-day Hindu festival celebrating the victory of the goddess Durga over a demon)

October/November—*Tihar* (five-day feast to honor the goddess of wealth, Laxmi)

FLAG DESCRIPTION

Two red overlapping right triangles with a blue border. The upper triangle is smaller and contains a stylized white crescent; the lower triangle contains a white 12-pointed sun.

TIME LINE

IN NEPAL	IN THE WORLD

Seventh and sixth century B.C
The Kiranti settle the eastern hills and Kathmandu Valley. The Buddha is born in Limbini.

753 B.C.
Rome is founded.

116–17 B.C.
The Roman Empire reaches its greatest extent, under Emperor Trajan (98-17).

A.D. 200
The Licchavi from northern India overthrow the Kiranti and establish a sophisticated kingdom.

A.D. 600
Height of Mayan civilization

879
The Thakuri overthrow the Licchavi; general decline for three centuries.

1000
The Chinese perfect gunpowder and begin to use it in warfare.

1200
The Malla Dynasty rises in Bhaktapur and spreads to other cities in the Kathmandu valley; five centuries of great cultural advancement follow.

1364
Muslim raiders from Bengal take over Kathmandu Valley.

1482
Yaksha Malla dies; the kingdom is divided among his three sons.

1530
Beginning of trans-Atlantic slave trade organized by the Portuguese in Africa.

1558–1603
Reign of Elizabeth I of England

1620
Pilgrim Fathers sail the Mayflower to America.

1768
After 25 years of fighting, Prithvi Narayan Shah captures and unifies Kathmandu valley.

1775
Prithvi Narayan dies; his successors expand the kingdom east and west.

1776
U.S. Declaration of Independence

1814
Nepal comes into conflict with the British East India Company; war breaks out.

1789–99
The French Revolution

1816
War with Britain ends with the Treaty of Seaguli.

IN NEPAL	IN THE WORLD

1846

Decades of court intrigue lead to Kot Massacre. Jang Bahadur Rana seizes power as prime minister and sets up a ruling dynasty that lasts for one century.

1857

Nepalese troops assist the British in the Great Mutiny; Britain returns lands in the *terai*.

1861
The U.S. Civil War begins.

1869
The Suez Canal is opened.

1914
World War I begins.

1939
World War II begins.

1945
The United States drops atomic bombs on Hiroshima and Nagasaki.

1950

Nepali Congress Party leads revolts and King Tribhuvan dismisses the Rana prime minister.

1949
The North Atlantic Treaty Organization (NATO) is formed.

1959

Nepali Congress Party wins the first free elections; B.P. Koraila becomes prime minister.

1957
The Russians launch Sputnik.

1960

King Mahendra seizes power.

1966–69
The Chinese Cultural Revolution

1990

King calls for elections after violent protests.

1986
Nuclear power disaster at Chernobyl in Ukraine

1991

G.P. Koirala becomes prime minister.

1991
Break-up of the Soviet Union

1996

Maoists in western Nepal start violent attacks.

1997
Hong Kong is returned to China.

2001

Crown Prince Dipendra kills most of the royal family, then himself; King Birendra's brother, Gyanendra, becomes king; government and Maoist groups hold talks, but no settlement is reached.

2001
World population surpasses 6 billion.

GLOSSARY

asylum
Refuge provided by a country to people fleeing political persecution.

bhaat ("bhaht")
Cooked rice.

bio-gas
Gas fuel obtained from decaying organic matter such as sewage and plant crops.

chiya ("chye")
Nepali aromatic tea, made with milk and spices.

creosote
An oily, strong-smelling liquid obtained from distilled coal and wood tar. It is used to preserve wood.

dal ("dahl")
A thick lentil soup, served at almost every Nepali meal.

hierarchy
A system which places people or things one above the other.

khukuri ("KHOO-koo-ree")
Nepali knife characterized by a curved blade and considered a national symbol.

Mahabharata
One of the two great Hindu epics, it recounts the heroic struggle of five brothers against their five evil cousins. (See Ramayana)

monsoon
A season marked by heavy rains caused by southwesterly winds in India and Southeast Asia.

namaste ("neh-MEHS-tay")
The traditional greeting and farewell, spoken with hands clasped together.

puja ("POO-jah")
The act of worshiping a Hindu deity.

prasad ("prah-SAHD")
The blessing, usually in the form of food and flowers, received after finishing a puja.

Ramayana
The other great Hindu epic, it recounts the adventures of the great hero Ram.

stupa
A traditional Buddhist structure; a hemispheric mound topped with a spire.

thangka ("TAHNG-kah")
Tibetan paintings with Buddhist themes, usually done on small- or medium-sized paper.

tika ("TI-kah")
A mark of blessing on the forehead, symbolizing the third eye of wisdom and inner knowledge, usually made with red powder.

Vedas
The Hindu scriptures dating back to 2000 B.C.

FURTHER INFORMATION

Books

Connell, Monica. *Against a Peacock Sky*. New York: Penguin Books, 1991.

Finlay, Hugh and Richard Everist. *Lonely Planet Nepal*. Melbourne: Lonely Planet, 2001.

Hutt, James (ed.). *Himalayan Voices: An Introduction to Modern Nepali Literature*. Berkeley: University of California Press, 1991.

Kipp, Eva. *Bending Bamboo, Changing Winds*. Delhi: Faith Books, 1995.

Mackenzie, Vicki. *Reincarnation: the Boy Lama*. Somerville: Wisdom Publishers, 1996.

Stephenson, Joanne. *Decision: The Story of Kumar, a Young Gurung*. Varanasi: Pilgrims Publishing, 2001.

Taylor, Irene. *Buddhas in Disguise: Deaf People of Nepal*. San Diego: Dawn Sign Press, 1997.

Tenzing Norgay, Jamling. *Touching My Father's Soul: A Sherpa's Journey to the Top of Everest*. San Francisco: Harper, 2001.

Websites

Central Intelligence Agency World Factbook (select Nepal from the country list) www.odci.gov/cia/publications/factbook/index.html

Country Reports (select Nepal from country list). www.countryreports.org

Gateway to Nepal. www.nepalsearch.com

Lonely Planet World Guide (Select destination region, Asia and destination country, Nepal) www.lonelyplanet.com/destinations

National Geographic Maps of Nepal. www.nationalgeographic.com/mapmachine

Nepal's newspapers and magazines. www.nepalnews.com

Radio Nepal. www.catmando.com/news/radio-nepal/radio.htm

Videos

Everest. Miramax, 1998.

Nepal: Land of Gods. Mystic Fire Studios, 1987.

Night Train to Kathmandu. Paramount Pictures, 1993.

BIBLIOGRAPHY

Anderson, Mary M. *Festivals of Nepal.* New Delhi, India: Rupa & Co., 1977.

Burbank, John. *Culture Shock! Nepal.* Singapore: Times Editions, 1997.

Central Intelligence Agency World Factbook. www.odci.gov/cia/publications/factbook/index.html

Dor Bahadur Bista. *People of Nepal.* Kathmandu, Nepal: Ratna Pushtak Bhandar, 1980.

Gateway to Nepal. www.nepalsearch.com

Nepal Home Page. www.info-nepal.com

Pye-Smith, Charlie. *Travels in Nepal.* London, England: Aurum Press, 1988.

Reed, David. *Nepal: The Rough Guide.* New York: Rough Guides Publishing, 1999.

INDEX